GOD HATES RELIGION

How the Gospels Condemn
False Religious Practice

GOD HATES RELIGION

How the Gospels Condemn False Religious Practice

CHRISTOPHER LEVAN

THE UNITED CHURCH PUBLISHING HOUSE

Copyright © 1995 The United Church Publishing House

All rights reserved. No part of this book may be reproduced, stored in a retrieval system, or transmitted, in any form or by any means electronic, mechanical, or otherwise, without the written permission of The United Church Publishing House.

All Gospel quotations are taken from the Scholars Version translation. *The Complete Gospels: Annotated Scholars Version.* Copyright © 1992, 1994 by Polebridge Press. Used with permission. All rights reserved.

Canadian Cataloguing in Publication Data

Levan, Christopher, 1953-
    God hates religion

Includes bibliographical references.
ISBN 1-55134-045-3

1. Church Renewal. I. Title.

BV600.2.L48 1995   262'.001'7   C95-932216-7

The United Church Publishing House
3250 Bloor Street West
Etobicoke, Ontario, Canada
M8X 2Y4

Book Design: Department of Graphics and Print Production
Printed in Canada

To Kelly Higgins,
never satisfied with simple answers;
and Brian Goodings,
never satisfied with easy questions.

Contents

Acknowledgements	viii
Prologue	xi

Introduction	
Can the Church be Revived?	1
Chapter 1	
Divine Irony and Blind Righteousness	17
Chapter 2	
The Subversive Minority Movement	29
Chapter 3	
Itinerant or Establishment Church?	44
Chapter 4	
The Church:	
Centrifugal or Centripetal Force?	59
Chapter 5	
Sin as a State of Being	74
Chapter 6	
Respectability and Other Hidden Boundaries	88
Chapter 7	
Just Us versus Justice	103
Chapter 8	
Puritanism, Legalism, and Apocalypticism	112
Chapter 9	
Retributive Transcendence Meets	
Extravagant Immanence	128
Chapter 10	
The Inverting Principle	139
Chapter 11	
Safe Church or Risking Church?	149

Bibliography	156

Acknowledgements

Many persons have knowingly or unknowingly offered assistance in the production of this book. The idea of it first arose in the Bible study classes that I was privileged to conduct at Centenary-Queen Square United Church in Saint John, New Brunswick. Never has a more eager and probing group of believers gathered, at least in my experience, and our many debates form the basis for the chapters that follow. All of the group members deserve an honourable mention, and I list them here in no particular order: Miggie, Marjorie, Billie, Edith, Margaret, Margo, Elaine, Troy, Brian, George, Linda, Lynne, Peggy, Helen, Tom, Gord, Lillian, Greta, Jeannie, May, Dorothy, Betty, Shirley, Susan, Angie, Scott, Margie, Alex, Derek, Gwen, Barb, Vilas. Thank you all!

The dedication and sincerity of these individuals is true of their church as a whole. I will always be grateful for the many gifts I received from the congregation of Centenary-Queen Square: the time and space to write, the honesty to tell me when my ideas needed more thought, and the graciousness to encourage me when I seemed to be going in the right direction.

My experience of parish ministry leads me to believe that, besides the faithful, who have many pressing questions, there are also some starved skeptics living on the edges of religion. These inquirers have a strong appetite for truth and sense that there is more to life than the detached, objective explanations suggested by our secular society. They long to see God, whoever or whatever that may be, and yet they can never quite join in the Sunday morning song and dance. I would be remiss if I did not acknowledge that it was my acquaintance with these people on the periphery that prompted my research into the nature of "false" religion. This book is an attempt to respond to the probing questions of these searchers.

When I think back over my years of Bible exploration, I see the faces of three student interns who have both delighted and challenged me. Elaine Hall, Troy Van Ginkel, and Brian Good-

ACKNOWLEDGEMENTS

ings have stretched my heart, mind, and soul, each in their own way. There is no more exacting stimulus to writing than the relentless questioning of fellow travellers.

Given the subject matter of this text, I wish to honour my father, Victor Levan. With him as my teacher, the Bible was never a dry subject. Many of my friends found it to be a dusty and dull collection of outlandish, insignificant ideas when compared, for instance, with "Hockey Night in Canada" broadcasts. But the Bible in our home was well thumbed. I found it be full of colour and texture, with a surprise waiting on every page. Since I can remember, my dad would open up its mysteries, tell the "old, old story" and unravel a host of questions. Even now, he still tests my intuitions and disarms me with his bold assertions. More recent mentors in biblical research are Daniel Fraikin and Bill Morrow, both excellent scholars and sympathetic teachers.

Two companions and fellow conspirators in many joint ventures deserve a good deal of credit for encouraging me to write. Peter and Bronwen Woods (the St. Martin's Collective) have been a constant source of inspiration, laughter, and understanding. Bronwen has been more than a friend in editing this text with a relentless and critical eye.

As always, Peter Gordon White and Elizabeth Phinney have given some very direct advice in the refinement of the central ideas of this work with a mixture of gentleness and down-to-business clarity. Dolores Bell, a great assistant in my work at St. Stephen's College, has put her considerable skill into proofreading the final manuscript.

Finally, I wish to thank Kelly Dawn Higgins, my partner. It is her patience and encouragement that affords me the opportunity to write and her lively spirit that has enabled me to risk vulnerability and play with abandon.

Technical Notes

The translation used for most of the gospel quotations in this text is the *Scholars Version*, written by the scholars of the Jesus

GOD HATES RELIGION

Seminar. It is cited as "SV" and is contained in its entirety in *The Complete Gospels: Annotated Scholars Version*, edited by Robert J. Miller (Santa Rosa, California: Polebridge Press, 1992, 1994). The *Scholar's Version* represents a very creative approach to the tradition of gospel translation. The authors have rendered the Greek words with a contemporary flavour, eschewing the more traditional phraseology. In addition, they have endeavoured to re-create the tone of the original writer. Hence, Mark, whose facility in Greek was poor, sounds a bit vulgar, while Luke sounds eloquent and smooth. When I refer to books of the Bible other than the Gospels, I will employ the New Jerusalem Bible (NJB).

I have made some provision for those who would like further reference material. When I rely on the scholarship of another author, I cite his or her name and give a page reference, if that is applicable. Such citations will correspond to the books listed in the bibliography.

Prologue

> *To everything there is a season, and a time for every thing under heaven.... A time to pull down and a time to build up; a time to weep and a time to laugh.*
>
> —Ecclesiastes 3:1,3b-4a, NJB

The Conversation of Belief and Unbelief

Late at night, when doubts dance with the shadows on the ceiling, I have a conversation with myself. Well, actually, it's more like a quarrel. "Belief" stands resolutely in one corner, ready to defend faith to the last gasp of my wheezing spirit. In the other corner, "Unbelief" waits with calm nonchalance, confident of the cynical barbs it has prepared to thrust into the side of organized religion. These nocturnal debates can rage for hours, with "Belief" always taking the initiative:

"I believe in God the Creator of all life, an extravagant Lover of my soul, and, therefore, I am proud of the noble accomplishments and courageous dreams of my religious tradition."

"I unbelieve in the All-powerful God. How can such a Being exist when so much pain and injustice holds sway on earth? All too often I am dismayed by what is done and said in the name of God."

"But isn't religion a restorative, green pasture for the wayward human soul? Like starved and lost sheep, all human beings return to it whenever they are in distress."

"Even as its essential goodness is outlined, I am reminded of the fundamental weaknesses of religious practice. There is a hollow sentiment which passes for love; the soul-destroying condescension of Christian charity, and the pompous piety of the priestly. I cannot fail to notice the shallowness of faith that masquerades as devotion. Consequently, my skepticism has grown over the years, settling easily on my shoulders. It's second nature by now, and I wear the mantle of a perpetually doubting Thomas."

"Yet, I'm also a minister of religion; have been for most of my life. Didn't I even dress up as a minister for Hallowe'en when I

GOD HATES RELIGION

was seven? Ask me if I'm a zealot! My belief is not so much the result of my own virtue as it is the influence of the faithful witnesses, the understated, unrecognized disciples of Christ that I have encountered. I'm not prepared to ignore their testimony of compassion and courage ... not yet."

"But have I not muttered that religion was 'for the birds'? Frankly, it has been hard to retain my child-like trust in religious ideals. After years of church work and ecclesiastical acrimony (indeed, my whole life has been given to institutional religion), I am now more inclined to see its blemishes than its triumphs.

To be honest, there is much about religion that is regrettable, almost laughable. Take the Sunday service, for example. When was the last time I was fed by it—nourished in my soul? Then there's the intolerable myopia of Christian policies and politics that focus on theological minutiae while the hungry starve and the captives are tortured. Piety, the popular variety now sold by North American evangelists, is pretty hard to stomach. We're so brittle and somber during our most solemn sacraments that I want to burst out laughing. In its present form, religion strains the limits of credulity."

"Nevertheless, while I could reject much of what masquerades as religion and leave it without a backward glance, there are some small miracles; moments when eternity breaks into existence with a stunning power. A woman in the line at the soup kitchen thanks God for the compassion of other Christians who supply her daily bread. A world traveller recounts how the best hospitals in Africa are still run by missionaries. A political activist from El Salvador recalls how she was released from prison and torture because of the efforts of the international church community."

"Its accomplishments notwithstanding, I remain unconvinced. Religion is a mistake, a dead end, a misguided error perpetuated by the frailty of human existence."

"Yes, it can be mistaken and in error. I am constantly surprised by the Scriptures, or more precisely, by the Christian Gospels; they too see the cracks in the smiling facade of religion; they too express a deep anger over ritualistic stupid-

PROLOGUE

ity and blind piety that preens itself before the Lord. It could be that one of the central messages of the Bible is: "God hates that form of false religion."

"'God hates religion' — I like that."

And so the argument continues, back and forth, round and round, with no easy resolution. Perhaps devotion to God is richer when it is coloured by strenuous doubt.

Many people on the fringe of religion, and even those within the churches, sense that their faith could be much more; that it is crippled by the frailty and disappointments of institutional religion. I myself am in that group, and it is for those who are frustrated or even ashamed of the established church that I have written this book. As the gospel's condemnation of false religion is outlined, perhaps we who yearn for a new community of faith will find a fresh vessel to catch the ever-flowing stream of our hopes.

xiii

Introduction

Can the Church be Revived?

The principle to be kept in mind is to know what we see rather than see what we know.

—Heschel 1962, xi

God may not be dead, but the church, Christ's body on earth, looks like it is in need of palliative care. The signs of the church's decay are so evident that it is difficult to dismiss a foreboding unease. Is the last decade of the twentieth century witnessing the decline of the religious enterprise? Can the church be revived or must it essentially die in order to make room for new life?

When I see the proud Christian structures that grace the town squares across this continent, buildings that stand vacant most of the time, even on Sunday mornings, I think of the cycles of nature and the inevitability of death.

Has anyone ever seen a forest grow into old age? Given its life span, it is difficult for human beings to witness a forest's entire cycle, for who lives for three hundred years or more? Our disrespectful clear cutting of old growth timber may stem from our lack of appreciation for the years it takes for a stand of trees to mature.

Imagine you are standing on a barren piece of land with not a shrub in sight. How will the typical forest grow? Through what stages will it progress? In rough terms, a forest grows in this fashion: Initially, small bushes, alders and thick grasses cover

1

the thin topsoil. Then as years pass, and as the spent foliage becomes rich fertilizer, other soft woods begin to dominate— poplar, white birch, spruce. Pine trees are quick to creep into the territory and out-distance the poplars. These soft woods spread quickly over the land, taking the precious sunlight from the smaller, weaker trees. But evergreens cannot endure forever. Cracking of limbs and trunks, storms, and infestations take away their strength. Eventually the slow-growing yet sturdy maples, oaks, and yellow birch begin to rise up. They've been growing quietly, patiently, on the forest floor, awaiting sufficient space. A hemlock topples, and suddenly these thumb-sized hardwood stocks take off, rising up into the life-giving light.

Over time, and if we lived long enough, we would see what is known as a climax forest — largely hardwood, dominated by one species or another. When a forest matures into its geronto-logical state dominated by maples, for example, inevitably a disaster will wipe the slate clean and the growth cycle will begin over again with small bushes and undergrowth. In the present context, this disaster most often takes the form of a fire or clear cutting. Like human beings, the older a forest becomes, the more susceptible it is to danger. It is inevitable; death is implicit within the life cycle of creation. Death follows life.

And as with forests, so with churches. For there are fires lurking ahead—disasters that spell the end of this species of community, at least as we know it. While many signs point to the imminent demise of the institutional church, three seem most dominant and menacing. We Christians must know them well before we can imagine the possibilities of new growth beyond the destructive flames that lie in their path. They are: (1) the reversal of roles between mainstream churches and radical sects in North American Christianity; (2) the decline and shift in membership of the older, traditional denominations; and (3) the general mediocrity of much Christian thinking and acting.

CAN THE CHURCH BE REVIVED?

Fire 1: The Great Reversal

Recent studies (see Bibby's two books in the bibliography and his survey on The United Church of Canada) indicate that the "classic," liberal, North American denominations are declining, at least numerically. Once proud bodies of the vocal majority, they appear as mere shadows of their former greatness, retaining an outward appearance of status, but inwardly confused and uncertain. In contrast, the membership of the fundamentalist churches, those we used to refer to in a pejorative light as the "fanatical fringe," remains constant or is increasing in numbers. There can be little doubt that the fundamentalist churches are overtaking the old mainline churches, both in size and influence. In a great role reversal, the sects are now centre stage, while the once-dominant churches have been pushed into the wings. Indeed, it now seems evident that the secular world more readily equates Christianity with its neo-conservative manifestations than with the older, liberal models. With the possible exception of the pope, evangelists like Jerry Falwell, Billy Graham, and Hal Lindsey are recognized as the official Christian voice.

This shift in status may not, in and of itself, be cause for lament. The quest to be the largest and most influential religion on the continent may constitute an empty endeavour, a distortion of the original purpose of the Jesus movement. Moreover, I doubt whether a church founded on the prophetic tradition of Jerusalem can survive as a faithful body and at the same time be granted privilege within the "Washington empire." Playing the role of chaplain to presidents and prime ministers drastically blunts the critical edge of Christian proclamation. Majority status with its concomitant political acceptability becomes a theological muzzle; the shortcut to a bland "Bless everyone, do nothing" discipleship.

Nevertheless, the shift by which the sect becomes church and the church devolves into a sect signals a subtle and, I believe, regrettable movement from moderate openness to guarded de-

3

GOD HATES RELIGION

fensiveness. Where the philosophical and political world could once debate questions of consequence with a relatively open-minded church, the reigning posture of right-wing theology precludes secular debates. At the extreme, the fundamentalist sees any intellectual discourse that leads to doubt as a tool of the devil and any ambiguity as a sign of spiritual weakness. Of course, all expressions of Christian thought are faulty and prone to ideological distortions, liberalism no less than any other. But the ascending sectarian religion is less capable of tolerating difference than were the former dominant models of Christianity and not as willing to compromise for the sake of a healthy common good.

Out of the best of intentions, these burgeoning sects are more concerned with the establishment of ecclesiastical purity than social equality; more exercised over individual spirituality than structural injustice. While the care and nurture of the soul is important, an "official" religion that is focused on personal, internal issues but has no serious regard for the health of the world is easily manipulated by political forces seeking to promote their own agenda. Recent elections in the United States give ample testimony to this phenomenon.

Moreover, it is evident from the Sunday shopping debate, the abortion conflict, and the school prayers issue that some of the more radical conservative believers feel no qualms about imposing their lifestyle and moral values on non-believers. "It's a Christian country after all!" Such innocent naiveté can mask a heavy-handed, often unthinkingly moralistic homogeneity, which attempts to re-impose Christendom ethics on an increasingly pluralistic society.

I believe the time has passed when one religious community could assert its will on the North American world. Accommodation will have to be made for many faiths. As secular forces and spiritual traditions resist the imperialism of the Christian right, they, in turn, may be prone to a shriller, less self-critical reactionary stance—a recipe for social unrest.

I was in Brussels recently, relaxing in the main square, enjoying an espresso and marvelling at the richness of the surrounding architecture. The plaza was filled with thousands of tourists and citizens, all doing the same thing. Suddenly, an American voice burst over this scene. As Belgium is proudly bilingual, Flemish and French, it was a surprise to hear English. Everyone in the plaza turned to look at the speaker, who was a remarkable sight—blonde, wild-eyed, defiant, violently gesturing with his arms. It was impossible to ignore his dramatic presence. As he continued to speak, it became evident that he was preaching, telling us all to "get right with God" and "accept Jesus as our Lord and Saviour." In response, there were a few annoyed expletives and quizzical frowns, and then everyone went back to their coffee. For only a few had understood the fire-breathing evangelist, and those few were embarrassed. After an initial glance, almost everyone ignored him.

I don't believe the young man recognized his own folly in speaking in a language that was neither comprehensible nor associated with the home culture. Does Christianity have the right to barge into other worlds, other cultures, and assume that its answers correspond to other people's questions? Will this be the parable for Christianity's role in the next century?

As the claims and counter-claims of special interest groups, races, and religions become more complex, an unbending, unreflective, ascendant form of Christianity is particularly inappropriate. For how can our world achieve a semblance of peace and mutual understanding when one of its major spiritual traditions wraps itself in isolation and fosters antagonism through its own arrogance and conceit?

If the tone and texture of its voice does not change, disaster awaits the entire Christian project. While such a threat is poised from outside the old-style Protestant churches, there is an even more serious problem within.

GOD HATES RELIGION

Fire 2: The Decline and Shift in Membership of the "Old" Churches

Similar to many service clubs and social institutions, the traditional mainstream churches are suffering, not only from a decline in membership, but from a shift in the type of persons who adhere themselves to the organization.

The church where I most recently served as a pastor is an excellent example. One hundred and fifty years ago, trusting and believing Methodists built a sanctuary to hold eleven hundred people. Such great expectations! Throughout both World Wars, all the spaces were filled. But with the migration to the suburbs and the disillusionment of the seventies and eighties, the pews emptied with a regularity that defied every style of leadership or liturgy. Now its members' average age is well over seventy, with 25 percent of the church family over eighty years of age.

Even though this is a slightly exaggerated picture when applied to the entire denomination, general trends are accurate. Loyal, aging members are dying. They take with them their financial support and, more importantly, their lifetime love affair with the church. These folk served long and hard, ensuring the continuance of their precious holy place.

In the centre of small towns and large cities, you can see their monuments, testimonies to the greatness of a former generation's faith. Now these buildings are millstones, draining liberal denominations of much-needed financial and spiritual energy. Rather than putting economic and physical resources into mission, they have all been spent on keeping the Sunday doors open.

In spite of this bleak picture, there are indications that new life is waiting to emerge. At the same time as many older members are dying, new, young families are finding their way back to church. Not a wave, not perhaps even a ripple, but some thinking people are giving institutional religion a second glance. Members of two-career families with active social commitments

CAN THE CHURCH BE REVIVED?

and countless other obligations cannot give their undivided attention to the church. Nevertheless, they are seeking some spiritual depth, tentatively at first, but desirous of substance and purpose for their lives.

Often these newcomers lack the same sense of belonging to a particular building or denomination as their parents had. Having grown up in a generation of abundance and seemingly infinite selection, there is no ultimate loyalty or faithfulness for this generation. This circumstance presents both opportunity and danger. For the first time in a long time, people are attending church without preconceived notions. A fresh "Why not?" breeze is blowing down the aisles. At the same time, some recent adherents look upon religion as a consumer product, and at themselves as purchasers of the right faith community for their children.

There is, of course, nothing wrong with selecting a church to suit one's tastes, but such a motivation could warp the spiritual enterprise as churches strive to appeal to these "shoppers." Religious leaders might fashion their services to respond to the perceived wishes of these new members in hopes of establishing a stable membership base and consequently undermine the critical and prophetic edge of faith.

If we return to the analogy of the forest, it could be argued that the older churches, like declining species of trees, are being surpassed. It may be that only a few archaic jack pines are in danger and not the entire forest. Isn't it possible that a new, unannounced reformation is passing through the old-style North American Protestant communities? Away with life-long traditions and unquestioning loyalty, with obligations of stewardship and high expectations of a morally binding code of ethics. Ring in the age of a user-friendly faith where the pretense of piety is lost; a time of short-term church adherence where membership is directly linked to services rendered. Herald in a new age of an unorthodox mix of secular and sacred thinking. It could well be an exciting, chaotically creative moment in the life of the church. One thing is certain—it won't be business as usual.

7

GOD HATES RELIGION

In spite of these possibilities, the once-mainstream churches have become, in reality, marginalized precisely because ours is not a religion that is inviting and responsive to the felt needs of ordinary people. This leads us to the third danger facing the classic expressions of Protestantism—mediocrity.

Fire 3: The Mediocrity of Much "Christian" Thinking and Acting

It was my honour to attend the annual AIDS memorial service hosted by the church where I worked. The local AIDS organization found the gothic architecture and good acoustics well-suited to their purposes.

And what a service it was. There was no doubt that we were engaged in the deepest of religious acts as we confronted death and suffering, grief and anger. A potent mixture. I was stunned by the sheer depth of spiritual insight displayed by those who otherwise did not attend worship services. The quality of the music, liturgical action, participation, and theological inquiry was astounding. We touched the holy and entered into the realm of the eternal.

It is no surprise that these very same people do not give "regular" church a second glance. Who would tolerate the Sunday morning mediocrity, the droning prayers devoid of feeling, the lack of spiritual passion in our music and sacraments, the general absence of spiritual realism and vitality?

Of course, it's not only a question of what the church lacks. It's also what we, as a religious organization, have. Returning members come through the doors, and what they see reinforces why they left—sloppy, psycho-theological babble that passes for preaching; archaic, parched music whose spring, alas now dried up, comes from the piety of past centuries; images of God as a scolding parent; and exhortations to be "good." Empty "beliefulness" is preached from the pulpit, and a tired indifference is the response from our pews.

Thinking outsiders see no serious engagement of their world, of the dark shadows that confront them. Where is the church seriously confronting the powers that touch their lives, the tensions of underemployment, the vacuousness of a consumer-driven society, the creeping, crippling restrictions of financial restraint? How does anything we say or do on a Sunday morning relate to the worldly concerns of the rest of week? Yes, this is an old complaint—timeless, and still true.

Those who are desperate, poor, and lost ask if there is anything that would cause a church to risk change, apart from its own survival. Would a community of faith have an enlightened approach to social issues and transform itself for the sake of the powerless? The seeming intransigence of the church leads outsiders to leave our buildings shaking their heads. Nothing has changed.

At the Roots

These are harsh criticisms. They do not apply to all North American churches equally or even to all classic expressions of Protestantism. Nevertheless, there is enough evidence of these dangers that it behooves us, as disciples, to think seriously about the root principles that shape and sustain our communities of faith. It may well be that the church was and is a colossal mistake and not at all what our Saviour had in mind. While the followers of Jesus have been fighting an institutional conflict, trying to build and secure a future through a lasting tradition, it is possible that this very process of institutionalization has corrupted or deformed the original intent of Christ's mission. Perhaps an exploration of the earliest Christian records will reveal quite a different organization and structure for believers.

The Christian Gospels do, indeed, testify to a "fitting" structure for Christian discipleship, one which the author of the Acts of the Apostles, for example, calls "the Way." While visions of this first "church" vary from gospel to gospel, there is no question that an early composite picture still looks and feels and thinks and acts differently from the present institution. Mat-

GOD HATES RELIGION

thew, Mark, and Luke portray their Saviour as a subversive preacher who is constantly confronting the religious establishment. In continuity with the prophetic dimension of the Hebraic faith from which it arises, the Christian Scriptures declare that "God hates religion," or at least abhors the version of establishment faith that falsifies reality and oppresses the powerless.

Jesus spent a considerable amount of his ministry condemning the very religious practice that now characterizes our Sunday devotions. The carpenter from Galilee certainly criticized any piety that adopted artificial righteousness, pretended to know God's mind, or so "routinized" the act of worship that it failed to heal the broken heart. Jesus opposed the self-serving use of religious festivals, the demeaning benevolence of "good" people, any priestly superiority, and false barriers of purity and class that separate believers.

Faithfulness lies in the constant reformation of our practice and thought. Given the dangers I have outlined above, we who still see or who still desire to find purpose and meaning in the Christian story are called to begin anew; to become as children and listen to the voices of our harshest critics in the light of the gospel's insights, and seek to recast the life of the company of Jesus in a fresh way.

In this book, we will explore the original stories and parables of Jesus found in the first three Gospels. The Fourth Gospel, John, while it contains some unique material, has been excluded because it represents a second strata of Christian Scriptures, one more eloquently refined and theologically sophisticated. The first three, Matthew, Mark, and Luke, are "hot off the press" so to speak, if writing forty to fifty years after the events can be viewed as such. They capture some of the apocalyptic urgency and fresh potency of the early movement and, as I shall illustrate, some of the most severe criticisms ever levelled at religion by Jesus himself.

Each of the following chapters in this text addresses a specific criticism of the present institutional church, voiced by its modern, cultured despisers. They illustrate how the gospel narrative

10

has anticipated these concerns, often agreeing with some of the harshest condemnations of religion. For instance, chapter 3 examines the problem of the geographically and socially established church in comparison with the disestablished version for which Jesus seemed to be pleading, and asks if religion can ever be "established" and "prophetic" at the same time. Perhaps our unspoken doubts about church real estate are well founded, and it was never meant to be a fixed and settled community.

While the material in the eleven chapters is not exhaustive, it does touch on the major weaknesses undermining the community of faith at this time in the North American context.

Even though the Gospels can sting believers with their pointed attacks on religious practice, they can point to possible solutions as well. At the same time as one must listen with earnestness to the gospel criticism of our holy traditions, it is also possible to hear in the "good news" some words of hope to discern a path forward. Consequently, each chapter concludes with a vision for the future.

Guides for the Journey

In past decades, Bible study has suffered from bad press, but it is on the rebound. In recent years, the excitement caused by the Jesus Seminar and its attempts to recreate the historical reality of Jesus has whetted many a layperson's appetite. People both within the church and on the fringe want to know more. Nevertheless, in spite of the hunger there is some residual reluctance to enter into a serious examination of Scriptures. Many argue that they lack basic tools: How do I read this sacred text? What are the criteria to guide my questions?

While what follows is not an exhaustive list of aids to biblical research, I have outlined some general insights that have increased my appreciation of the gospel story. As this work links the work of theology and biblical studies, I trust the following principles will allay undue distress before the study commences.

GOD HATES RELIGION

1. Unless one wants to adopt a literalist reading of scripture, it is important to accept that the biblical record is not a history text. It was not written with anything near the rigour demanded of modern historians. On the contrary, the gospel writers were testifying to their faith in Jesus and only secondarily trying to give what modern critics would call a factual picture of his ministry.

   In the Bible, truth and fact are not always equal. This may seem strange at first, but consider this illustration. If the United Nations (U.N.) commissioned a statue for its New York headquarters that portrayed a circle of people from many ethnic backgrounds holding hands, we would declare that it was a "true" portrait of that organization. The U.N. does, indeed, bring many nations and races together in an unbroken human chain. But such a statue is not factual. This precise group of people did not meet and form a circle. So, too, the Gospels declare many things that are true, but which may have an unknown, distorted, or non-existent historical basis.

2. Our approach to the reading of the Gospels is further complicated by various "screens" that separate us from the actual events that the evangelists describe. For instance, it is largely agreed that Mark, likely not an eyewitness, wrote his Gospel first, around 70 C.E., some forty years after the crucifixion. Luke and Matthew, also recording at least second-hand knowledge, wrote their Gospels approximately ten years later. Other writings appeared after the actual events and before Mark's Gospel (the Gospel of Thomas, Paul's letters, for example), but much of this material is the result of at least twenty years of oral transmission. Such a long period of time could not but result in some distortion of the original message.

   Another major screen through which the material was filtered before it arrived in its present form is ecclesiastical in nature. For example, the church and the synagogue were just

CAN THE CHURCH BE REVIVED?

beginning to differentiate themselves from one another as Mark set stylus to papyrus. Hence, it is not surprising that many parables and sayings of Jesus were given a competitive or antagonistic spin. In the chapters that follow, the question of the ferocious debate between these two religions will arise numerous times.

3. Bible study, once it has left the purely technical areas of language and grammar, is a question of translation. How does one take a word from an ancient language, one which carries its own cultural, social, and spiritual freight, and make it comprehensible in our present context? There are three options. First, we can transliterate it—find the exact word in our language that corresponds to the ancient word. In many cases this is an excellent approach. The Greek word *kosmos* is translated quite adequately by the English phrase, "the ordered world."

However, there are some grave shortcomings in transliteration. For instance, we could translate the petition about forgiveness in the Lord's prayer as "Forgive us our loans, as we forgive those who have outstanding loans with us." This didn't make a lot of sense to the traditional religious mind, so we have spiritualized the meaning of the Greek original, turning "loans" into "debts," and hence into "trespasses." These slight shifts are the work of translation, the second option. Translation is the development of the same meaning in a foreign tongue, employing different words than the original text, but preserving the basic idea.

In many cases, translation is sufficient, but I would suggest there are moments when we need to "transcreate" a biblical word, phrase, or parable. In order to achieve the same meaning for our present context, we must abandon the literal words in order to recreate the original meaning as understood by its first listeners. Using the same example of the word "debts," it would be possible to argue that the disciples heard Jesus alluding in that second petition of the

13

GOD HATES RELIGION

Lord's prayer to the radical economics of the jubilee year found in the Hebrew Scriptures. In order to capture that meaning, we might pray, "Forgive us our mortgages, as we forgive those who have mortgages with us." Using modern concepts, the words create in us the same sensation, surprise, and consternation that they did for the people of Galilee.

I will employ this method of transcreation throughout the book. Thus, I do not claim that my words are always faithful to the exact words of the Greek, but that they are faithful to the original intention and meaning.

4. The mention of intention raises a thorny issue. Can anyone get into the mind of Jesus and establish what he really wished to say? Obviously, this is not a simple task.

From our historical distance, it is impossible to establish what Jesus intended for his individual spiritual renewal, or collective Judean reform movement, or church. Did he even expect anyone to develop a new organization at all? He was a Jew, preaching to Jews about a very Hebraic idea—the imperial reign of God. We do not know what he intended his listeners to do in structuring their response to his parables. Given the gap between the actual utterance and the recording of these sayings of Jesus, it is quite impossible to make firm pronouncements about Christ's intention for an organization of followers.

Nevertheless, one can match the meanings drawn from one parable with other phrases and see a pattern evolving. Accordingly, this book will try to draw a few broad sketches of what we might assume the early believers felt that Jesus wished. From the patchwork of stories touching on his healings, miracles, and prophetic acts, some of his expectations for his disciples can be gleaned. But all our best efforts notwithstanding, we will have to be satisfied with broad ideas of his original motives; ideas which themselves must be transcreated into modern form before they can be applied to institutional religion.

14

CAN THE CHURCH BE REVIVED?

5. I will not spend a great deal of time trying to discern what Jesus actually said. There are many scholarly books listed in the bibliography that tackle that problem. When possible, I have taken these scholars' best guesses and incorporated them into the text, giving due reference.

6. Even those with no prior experience of biblical stories can understand the arguments presented in this book. No matter what our level of academic training, we all have inklings of spiritual insight. There is no special knowledge necessary to think our way into God's presence. A willing heart and an open mind will do just fine. Therefore, I trust that the chapters that follow will act as an invitation for the reader to further explore and test his or her ideas.

    The one necessary skill in the reading of Scripture is the suspension of our assumptions. Even agnostics, who have grown up in a culture largely shaped by the Christian mindset, have preconceived notions of what the "Good Book" says. Many ideas that seem self-evident to us are, in fact, human constructs—the developments of Christian thinkers. Usually, we have no awareness of the filters through which we view the biblical text. Many, if not most, attempts to develop a re-reading of Scripture have fallen prey to the distortions of our unseen, culturally accepted assumptions.

    Our task will be to examine those assumptions closely and, as much as possible, to know what we see in the biblical text, rather than seeing what we already know. Here's an example. How many "wise men" are there in Matthew's account of the nativity? Our immediate response is automatic. Even the youngest among us knows there were three. We see all three at every Christmas pageant or arranged in our manger crèche. But the Gospel writer doesn't mention any specific number. There aren't even any "wise men." A closer translation might be "astrologer" or "astronomer/politician." I can't emphasize enough that our work is to know what we see, not see what we know.

15

GOD HATES RELIGION

Conclusion

I invite you to an exciting task, a breath-taking endeavour. Let us look at the "old, old story" with new eyes. Take time to hear its words again. Over the centuries, these ideas have transformed lives, subverted empires, and radically changed human self-understanding. Should we expect anything less for ourselves?

Chapter 1

Divine Irony and Blind Righteousness

For naïve idealists are always so preoccupied with their own virtue that they have no residual awareness of the common characteristics in all human foibles and frailties and could not bear to be reminded that there is a hidden kinship between the vices of even the most vicious and the virtues of even the most upright.

—Niebuhr 1952, 147

Hallowing Our Doubts

In our childhood, the sacred was present to us in a way that is lost to us as adults. In the spring season of our lives, we feel the eternal everywhere. Do you recall that bright morning in the school yard when you reached out for love from a friend and it came pouring back? Feeling at one with the world, you said to yourself (was it a prayer or a promise?), "God, it's good to be alive."

Belief was easy then, but you grew out of your infantile faith and nothing has replaced it. You may have left the church at the enlightened and disdainful age of twelve because it was boring or stupid or just plain old-fashioned. Aside from the odd visit at Christmas or Easter, which only served to reinforce your earlier suspicions of institutional religion, you have been quite comfortable in your non-practicing agnosticism.

Maybe you should stay as you are, trusting your doubts, for

GOD HATES RELIGION

there is something quite healthy and inspiring about unbelief. And contrary to what you might think, unbelieving is an essential step on the journey to lasting belief. Think about it. If I only believe, without testing my doubts and examining my fears, my faith is naught but an empty shell, a house of cards waiting to be blown over at the first sign of resistance. True belief grows from the struggle with doubt and unbelief.

Take sickness for example. When I am healthy, God is not as necessary or present to me as when I am ill. It is in moments of helplessness and darkness that I search most earnestly for answers and assurances. Without the doubt caused by ill health, I would not plead to find God with the same sincerity and seriousness.

Unbelieving is also a check against facile credulity. Not every doctrine or idea merits our belief. Some spirits are deceiving us. There once was a great religious thinker who, upon being asked by a reporter, "Do you believe in the devil?", replied, "No, never! I can't believe in the devil. He lies!"

Unbelieving is furthermore an entry into human frailty and, in a manner I do not fully comprehend, a pilgrimage towards God. I feel there is a pain within the heart of God, one caused by human cruelty and injustice. This pain cannot be approached by untroubled statements of belief. Rather, we catch a glimpse of the divine as we travel back and forth along the continuum between doubt and faith, as we wrestle with our virtue and cowardice. God is found, or perhaps it is more accurate to say God finds us, as we undertake that struggle. To use an analogy, the divine-human encounter is like a moving stream, not a static event. Unbelieving is the acknowledgement that we have no fixed address; we're always searching, plunging onward and taking our chances.

Since doubt is so common, it is understandable that the first defence people employ when they explain why they are no longer practicing members of a church is the supposed naiveté or duplicity of its members. We cringe as they say, "Oh, I was once interested, but the people are all such hypocrites. They

18

DIVINE IRONY AND BLIND RIGHTEOUSNESS

think they know it all, being so sure of their faith. With all my doubts, I couldn't stay." Alas, there are church people who can leave us with the distinct impression that they are either overly impressed by their own virtue or unaware of their culpability, unable to see the fault lines in their faith; "good" people who are unaware of how unrealistic their goodness has become.

In most circumstances, it is this perceived "holier than thou" pretence that is most grating to the outsider. For no one is surprised by failure. There isn't a human being alive who is free from broken dreams, relationships, and promises, or from the pain of doubting. It is the denial of human ambiguity that is difficult to accept; and doubly difficult when it is done in the name of piety and covered over with a thick layer of self-righteousness.

In theological terms, I would call this pretence the sin of pride. People are pretending to be more than they are, high above mortal failings. It is not a coincidence that this predicament seems to be the most common one which Jesus faced and about which the Gospels speak.

Pharisees: The Good People

Let us examine the story of the call of Levi, the tax collector, to disciplehood (Luke 5:27-32). Before examining the actual text, we need to understand two important dimensions of that world—the role of the Pharisees and the prevailing definition of sin.

When trying to understand the dynamics portrayed in the gospel stories, it is essential that we remind ourselves that Christ and his followers were mainly devout Jews. The early apostles were living through unique times. Extraordinary demands were made on their spiritual and intellectual sensitivities. They found themselves in a new situation—what we would call a fundamental paradigm shift. What did this Jesus mean? How should they begin to fashion and structure their belief in the Saviour? How to balance the old ideas and the fresh spirit sweeping the

GOD HATES RELIGION

hearts of faithful Jews? How to regard those who would have nothing to do with the carpenter from Galilee? Were they friend or foe?

The fledgling community of Christ, which may not have understood itself to be completely separate from the Jewish faith until late into the first century, was, nevertheless, trying to differentiate itself from its parent religion. There were no easy guidelines, and a good deal of animosity was created as the two faiths disentangled themselves. Political intrigue and interference didn't help matters much. And as the Jesus movement struck out on its own, the Pharisees were very clearly the competition. As Christianity gained power, these natural, if regrettable, antagonisms became lethal.

The ambiguous and difficult context within which the Gospels were written must be raised in order to explain the suspicious attitude towards the Pharisees found in the Christian Scriptures. We are called to look behind this cultural bias written into the Gospels in order to see the Pharisees for who they were. Until we have comprehended their essential role in our own life as believers and in the life of the society of Jesus, we have not touched the radical heart of the gospel.

The Pharisees were respected and honoured people. They were the kind of people we'd like to appoint to our church boards or have as godparents of our children. They were law-abiding citizens, models for all.

In many respects, the Pharisees represented the best of Judaism at that time. Until their revitalizing movement, most worship was concentrated in central temple cults. People wishing to "get right with God" had to travel to these centres and perform certain ritual acts. They depended upon the good offices of priests for their salvation. Hence, religion was mediated; God was at arms-length. The Pharisees set about changing that by developing local centres of piety. They argued that a person could find purity through keeping the law, the Torah, in his or her own heart, and that a priest was not necessary for a relationship with God. Just honour the laws and God would be satis-

20

DIVINE IRONY AND BLIND RIGHTEOUSNESS

fied. This was surprisingly revolutionary thinking, not dissimi-
lar from the liberation of the Christian reform movement of
Martin Luther.

The Pharisees were innovative people. Nonetheless, the Gospels contain a very consistent animosity towards them. It has
been suggested that this anger reflects more on the context
within which the Gospels were written than on the historical
reality of Jesus' ministry. It may well be that the actual opposition to Jesus was from the priestly caste—scribes, levites, and
temple employees. It was, after all, this caste that felt his sting
most directly during the Passion Week sermons in Jerusalem,
for instance. They had the most to lose from a free-wheeling,
independent religious revival. Thus, in contrast to the historical
context of Jesus, the four evangelists' animosity to the Pharisees
may well reflect a post-resurrection phenomenon in which the
main opponents were the Pharisees. It would be natural enough
for the gospel writers to include some of the divisions and
polarities of their own day in their re-telling of the story of Jesus.

Whatever the source of the vilification of the Pharisees, it
seems that the Christian movement's criticism of pharisaism
centres largely on the legalism with which they kept the Torah—abiding by all the detail of its purity codes. In the Synoptic
Gospels, Pharisees are portrayed as the quintessential legalists.
This connection is so strong that it has even become part of the
English language. My dictionary lists the following definitions
of the word *pharisee*: "formalist; self righteous person; hypo-
crite" (Coulson 1969, 394).

While modern individualists may chafe at the seemingly restrictive injunctions the Pharisaic movement proposed, it is important to appreciate that the Pharisees' invocation of daily
rules was an innovation designed to free individuals and give
them a sense of control over their own religious practice. No
longer bound by the artificial hierarchy of purity imposed by
the temple cult, the Pharisees constructed a world in which
individuals could independently achieve a state of righteousness and purity.

GOD HATES RELIGION

The Pharisees were not the only people to re-define purity. Jesus was also quite revolutionary. Dominic Crossan suggests that pharisaic Judaism and Christianity are twin daughters of the parent religion—each an innovation, each competing for the heart of Jews. Arguments that began as in-house acrimony become more virulent and deadly as the two traditions separate and as one (Christianity) gains political power.

One of the dividing lines between these squabbling siblings was the question of purity. Jesus rejected the pharisaic understanding and introduced a paradigm shift in religious thinking. To recognize his innovative thought it is necessary to understand that sin was viewed quite differently by the people of his time than by modern believers.

The Nature of Purity

Essentially, the gospel equates sin with impurity. It's a wide generalization, but we could argue that, in the Bible, one's righteousness was dependent upon one's cleanliness. While purity was basically a physical quality, it also had spiritual dimensions, as there was no neat division between body and spirit as is the case today. Purity was not static; it was an achievement. Likewise, impurity was active, a contagious or defiling condition. Hence, religious acceptability was largely a question of keeping oneself free from contact with defiling objects or people, and not, as we currently define it, a matter of moral conscience or spiritual rigour. One's energies were spent avoiding those people and situations that would make sin "rub off." For instance, bodily fluids were considered defiling—blood, secretions of any kind, menstrual flow, semen—and made one unacceptable to God. Touching dead bodies was defiling, as was any communion with gentiles who were notoriously unconcerned with purity. Why else were there money-changers at the temple? They took the defiling money (Roman currency) and converted it into the pure temple coinage. A first-century homemaker's tasks included a round of household labours de-

22

signed to ward off defiling substances, preparing the proper foods, guarding against the uncleanliness proscribed in Leviticus. It was not easy to stay clean.

Besides fluids, defilement was associated with physical disfigurement. Anyone with a serious skin blemish or disease that deformed the body was deemed impure. It was argued that such obvious plagues were signs of God's displeasure.

Unlike our common, very North American assumption that sin is a matter of choice (i.e., we decide whether or not to do a sinful thing), the Hebraic mind saw impurity largely as a state of being. It was simply who you were. If you were a prostitute, for example, it didn't matter what you thought, did, or said. You were a *de facto* sinner because you touched gentiles, bodily fluids, or both. Moreover, you were a contagion, able to pass on your sinfulness to others. Is it any surprise that prostitutes in the gospel record felt liberated when Jesus declared they were forgiven their sins? Likewise, tax collectors were sinners, not only because they cheated or exploited the poor, but because of their contact with unclean gentiles. It didn't matter what a tax collector might do or say. They were outside the realm of the righteous.

With a renewed appreciation of the ancient contextual attitude to sinfulness and its immutable quality, imagine how Levi felt when Jesus asked him to be a disciple.

The Call of Levi

Feel the liberation of Jesus' teaching as he unbinds this religious straight-jacket, this understanding of sin, from an outcast's life. Here is Luke's version:

> *After these events he went out and observed a toll collector named Levi sitting at the toll booth. He said to him, "Follow me!" Leaving everything behind, he got up and followed him.*
>
> *And Levi gave him a great banquet in his house, and a large group of toll collectors and others were dining with them.*

GOD HATES RELIGION

> *The Pharisees and their scholars would complain to his disciples: "Why do you people eat and drink with toll collectors and sinners?"*
>
> *In response Jesus said to them: "Since when do the healthy need a doctor? It's the sick who do. I have not come to enlist religious folks to change their hearts, but sinners!" (Luke 5:27–32, SV).*

With all the urgency of a great, miraculous mission, Jesus calls business people from their offices. Without a backward glance, they leave their cashbooks and ledgers behind. Not unlike the fishers Peter and John, Levi responds immediately to the call. The fateful words, "Follow me," command instant obedience.

However, unlike the call of other disciples, Levi's acceptance of discipleship is coupled with a moralism. It is difficult to know if the "call" story was connected originally with a debate between Jesus and the Pharisees about sickness and health—a matter for other scholars. What we are interested in is the reaction of the "good" people. Jesus went off to a party with "bad," defiling people who were unfit because of their commerce with gentiles. They had touched tainted money and rubbed shoulders with unclean folk, especially the Romans who were also *personae non gratiae* because of their status as invaders. Could this be the messiah—eating and partying with sinners?

Imagine that you are in the first-century Christian community and you are trying to use Luke's story to convert your fellow Jews. Would it not sound to orthodox Judean ears that Jesus was breaking the rules, perhaps even flaunting them? Remember, these were rules which had an ancient tradition. Even at the time of Jesus, they had been hundreds of years in the making.

Jesus goes to eat with this crowd of sinners. *Eat* with them! How vile! Here is a wise man, the anointed one of God, sharing a meal with impure people. Eating meant dipping one's bread into the same dish as others in the circle, as there were no discrete portions available. One's hand went into the common bowl. Imagine! All *their* impurities mixed with the food you ate! To transcreate this scene, we would have to picture a fondue meal, with no long forks, shared with tuberculosis patients.

While the meal is not a central part of this story, it could be that Jesus used the fellowship of the table as the central means for conversion. For it is his table practice that precipitates the debate and allows Jesus or the gospel writer or both to make an important point about his messiahship. As you read Scripture, see the common meal as much more than a narrative convention. Whenever the reader encounters a meal scene in the Gospels, one is getting to the heart of Christ's mission.

I can't read this story of Levi without acknowledging the humorous side of the carpenter from Galilee. We so often read the Scriptures with a straight face, failing to hear the nuances, the subtle ironies, of the text. Listen again to the final verse: "In response Jesus said to them: 'Since when do the healthy need a doctor? It's the sick who do. I have not come to enlist religious folks to change their hearts, but sinners'"(SV). Now I will add a few words to illustrate the irony. When you read it aloud you can taste some of Jesus' wit: "In response, the Rabbi said to them: 'Since when do people who think they are healthy (people like you) need a doctor? No, no, it's only the people who know they are sick that need help. I have not come to enlist religious folk like yourselves, who are the good people, but only those others who are sinners.'"

Jesus was not that sardonic, but the point is that he is making fun of the presumption of righteousness. The "good" religious folk, those who are sure of their virtuous faithfulness, do not realize that they are sick because they can't imagine being anything but well. How could they possibly be in need of spiritual guidance, the healing of which Jesus spoke?

It is precisely because the religious people have a prestigious position in their world that they are unable to see their need of healing. Jesus is pointing to the irony of their pretence and, I believe, hoping that through this mild rebuke, this clever twist, they will gain insight into their own failings. We can hear this

GOD HATES RELIGION

text as a good-humoured invitation to create a revitalized, self-consciously honest community.

Jesus understood that being religious has a factory-installed flaw: one begins to believe one is not in need of the very spiritual discipline one claims to follow. You may have heard the devout going out the church door, saying, "I've been going to church all my life, and I don't need any new minister telling me what to do." Good people can be sadly out of touch with their spiritual well-being, unable to entertain a healthy scepticism regarding their own virtue. The righteous often need salvation and healing precisely because their righteousness has blinded them. The ones who know themselves and their brokenness are actually on the road to healing, while the people who believe they are well may be, in fact, sick.

This same pattern of knowing and not knowing one's spiritual state is expressed in very graphic terms in Matthew 25:31 and following verses. In the parable of the last judgement, Jesus speaks of how people can be indifferent to the need for charity and love. Their minds are so fixed on one dimension of divinity, that of a heavenly, detached Creator, that they cannot see the God who is at their side. In contrast, the people who have served God in their neighbour don't know themselves to be of any particular worth. Luke's parable of the good Samaritan contains a similar ironic reversal in which a "bad" person, a heretic, is actually the one who sees and acts righteously. In contrast, the "good" people, the ones who believe they are righteous, act abominably.

These are but three representative examples of a gospel theme that makes a very subtle, yet central, point concerning righteousness: Those people who think they are good, are not. If you want to uncover true righteousness, look for those who would deny they have it.

26

DIVINE IRONY AND BLIND RIGHTEOUSNESS

The Problem of Church Righteousness

Many persons on the fringe of religion are correct when they suggest that the institutional church is unattractive because its members profess to be more just, charitable, and holy than it is reasonable to be this side of God's reign. It is precisely this presumption of righteousness and pretence to blessed assurance that the Gospels condemn. In his day, Jesus confronted both spiritual pride that claimed more for itself than was reasonable and religious insiders who could not comprehend their own failings. And when Jesus was not trying to liberate the powerless from their burdens of guilt and ignorance, he was attacking the establishment religion (calling its leaders a "generation of vipers" at one point in Matthew 23:33), precisely because it thought it had the corner on God.

Religion is a balancing act between credo and confession, between "I believe" and "I doubt." When it devolves into unbridled belief, religion becomes a frightening weapon (Christian anti-Judaism being an apt example).

Among Protestant churches, it has often been assumed that the Calvinists were the most ardent in their pursuit of purity. One historian reports that he "would rather face an entire battalion of calvary with their swords drawn, than one lone Calvinist who believes he's doing the work of God." While Calvinists have dampened their enthusiasm, fear of the zeal of righteousness is still justifiable today. One has only to spend a few hours on the receiving end of Christian charity at the local food bank, for example, to feel the oppression of the "good" people.

The Healthy Church: A Circle of Laughter

If God is too vast and broad to be captured by any human pronouncement, and if those who claim to understand God or somehow embody the Godly lifestyle are mistaken, what is left? What shape does the unpretentious church take?

Imagine if the church became a circle of laughter, a holy place

GOD HATES RELIGION

where we learned to laugh at ourselves. In this company we would not take our piety and purity with such seriousness; we would loosen the tightness and pretence that has all too often coloured our creeds and communities.

As we pass through the portals of the next century, we may well need a sense of humour.

Chapter 2

The Subversive Minority Movement

I was brought up on the theory that in order to be prosperous, a country had to be big, the bigger the better.

—Schumacher 1973, 63

How Many? How Much?

As inevitable as spring flowers, each new year brings the church statistical forms. Designed with the best of intentions, these tally sheets reportedly keep the wider church informed of the status of its many small flocks scattered throughout the country and provide a wise and careful accounting of our Christian steward-ship.

Alas, the questions these forms pose are all too predicable. How many marriages? How many baptisms? How many funer-als? Did any new members join the church? Did the number of contributing members rise or decline? How many? How much? In my own denomination, aside from a page on the organiza-tion's officers and their addresses, the forms never pose qualita-tive questions. These quantitative queries deliver the questionable message that our discipleship is to be measured on the basis of numerical growth.

If this were the only instance of the numbers game, of Chris-tian growth spelled "b-i-g-g-e-r," we could disregard it as inci-dental to the real work of Christian ministry. Unfortunately, Christians within the North American context are hooked on

GOD HATES RELIGION

our culture's fascination with numbers and the potent drugs of grandeur and size. "How big is your church? How many people does it seat? How many contributing households? What's the size of the Sunday school?" When the first questions we ask of ourselves and our worship of God are number-oriented, it is clear we are preoccupied with a very narrow aspect of religious growth.

Do you ever hear believers talk about the depth of spiritual experience offered by their particular church? Rarely. Is the growth in ethical reasoning or theological discussion ever mentioned? Again, rarely. Things that can't be counted are largely ignored. The real and easiest measurement of Christian growth is the number of warm bodies in the pews on Sunday morning.

Let me suggest an experiment you might try. Ask your religious friends about their church. Make your query deliberately vague, something like, "Tell me about your home church." Listen to their reply. How quickly do they make use of mathematics in order to describe their community of faith?

How sad it is that rather than ask how close we came to transcendence (Did we touch the Spirit of God this Sunday morning?), we ask ourselves how many took communion. As we count the little "shot" glasses after service, we gauge our relative merit as a company of Christians. We assume that a full sanctuary is indicative of right doctrine instead of exploring the rightness or wrongness of faith statements, such as "What is the implication of a God who is detached in heaven?"

The measurement scales of our culture are mis-applied to church life. Although mass appeal is automatically proof of success and progress within secular society, it may be the opposite for Christ's company. When the latest mega-mall is built, the larger stadium completed, the populace is enchanted with our apparent progress. Why shouldn't this also apply to churches? It is only logical that the larger the building, the greater the glory will be to God. Isn't it? How often do old-style Protestants look down the street to the new, flashy cathedrals of right-wing evangelists and say to themselves, "They know what they're

30

THE SUBVERSIVE MINORITY MOVEMENT

doing." Here are the examples of what the church should be. Their large congregations are impressive, their buildings, breathtaking.

Let we who are church leaders be honest. Have we never asked ourselves, in the quiet corners of our doubt, "How do they do it? How do they fill the pews week after week?" And have we not thought, "They must have some gimmick"? Imagining they possess a secret power, we'd like to discover their "trick" and implement it as soon as possible.

Along with church reports, a new year brings an annual meeting, a public accounting. Of late, those of us whose churches are shrinking are inclined to lament that we must be doing something wrong. Can you hear our prayer? "O Lord, you see all. Look now upon our community and see that the Pentecostal church down the street is bursting with young families, and we are languishing." The obvious answer, unspoken of course, is that God is blessing them while punishing us.

Our dismay over our shrinking size is in direct contrast to the models Jesus used for the coming reign of God. Numerical success does not seem to be part of his formula for a rejuvenated faith. Nevertheless, the equation between popularity and God's blessing is part of the classic North American religious paradigm. Given that this notion influences so much of our theological and ecclesiastical practice, it deserves some amplification before we turn to the gospel itself.

At the time of the Enlightenment (the fifteenth century onward), humanist Christian philosophers purported that Homo sapiens were capable of improving themselves in co-operation with the Creator God. This theory was a revolutionary innovation. When contrasted with the strict determinism of medieval scholastics, the ideas of human potential for self-improvement and individual freedom were quite advanced notions.

Coincidentally, as the notion of a "new" humanity was developing through the efforts of great thinkers like Erasmus, a new world was discovered. Here was an opportunity, not just to talk the talk, but to walk the walk. The first white settlers of this

GOD HATES RELIGION

continent were religious folk, looking for a place to establish their faith communities based on a revised and improved image of humanity freed from the constraints of European pessimism. In this new land, Christians saw their chance to create a new Jerusalem, a place to flourish and grow strong without the grinding orthodoxy of state-run ecclesiastic bodies.

Here in this "New World," a new creation would be born, perhaps even the long-promised kingdom of God. It was extravagant thinking that spawned the birth of white civilization on this continent. And in the name of "enlightened" existence, white zealots invaded the land, killing Aboriginal peoples whom they thought inferior or primitive.

Along with their vision of a new social order, the early religious settlers brought a very "high" doctrine of God: the all-powerful, all-present, all-knowing deity, who ruled from above. This God was present in every facet of life; "God sees the little sparrow fall." There was nothing beyond God's grasp.

Given the constant growth of the white settlements and the seeming inexhaustible capacity for economic and technological expansion on this continent, it was widely assumed that chronological time was equivalent to salvation history. Every revolution marked by the hand of time was inextricably bound to the march towards the coming reign of God. Each new invention was heralded as "progress." Each dawning day brought welcome "advances" in science, in architecture, in almost all fields of human endeavour. Progress was inevitable; indeed, it was pre-ordained by God.

Now comes the great leap, the unique invention of the North American Christian world. If God is what we claim, omnipresent and all powerful, and if the world is constantly improving, then God must intend progress to be equivalent with time, woven right into the fabric of history. "Bigger and better" is not just an economic slogan or sociological premise; it is a divine fiat.

The idea is that progress is a function of time, building towards the accomplishment of God's eternal design. I call this

THE SUBVERSIVE MINORITY MOVEMENT

exaggerated preoccupation with God directing all things and being the all-manipulative deity "providentialism." It places God in a binding contract with a very suspect human construct of historical progress. Just as the European world erred in its bondage of human will, so North American providentialism may well be an equivalent bondage, of the Creator.

Given this theological climate, is it no wonder that formerly mainstream Protestants are crying in their communion cups. For if God is in control of everything within human time, and divine favour is linked to "progress," then smaller numbers and declining revenues must be indications of God's disfavour. Churches that can no longer demonstrate that they are "improving, growing, and expanding," must surely be forsaken by God. As we set our ecclesiastical course each new year, we feel like ship-wrecked sailors, set adrift without hope of rescue, no matter how often we sing "Amazing Grace."

The European tradition had a strong antidote to the disease of providentialism and the addictions it creates. Memories of plague or of endless wars cast doubts on the pristine picture of time as an ever-progressive march towards God's ultimate rule on earth. In contrast, North Americans have no memories prior to the age of progress, no prior visions by which to evaluate the shining dreams of a new land.

If we think of ideas in biological terms, the darkness of Europe was a natural predator of the shiny optimism of human self-improvement. Once the dream was transported to a land where there was check on its growth, it was free to run rampant. It has only been within recent decades, with a "revised" reading of the World Wars, the disillusionment of Viet Nam, the seemingly constant recession, the spectre of ethnic cleansing, the scourge of AIDS, and the rising jobless rate, that North Americans have had some taste of the shadow side of creation, well known elsewhere on the planet.

In spite of this brush with the darker side of creation, church leaders remain preoccupied with growth and size. Even in new church development circles, size and progressive increases in

GOD HATES RELIGION

membership are central, unquestioned values. While the addiction to grandeur may be a theological problem, it is also a stewardship issue. Energy put into keeping the doors open or finding enough people to make a church viable is energy drained away from a limited supply. The possession of real estate robs the church of valuable and revitalizing forces. Hence, there is little or none available for pressing spiritual and ethical matters.

Consider the wealth of dedication and well-meaning loyalty that is centred in fund-raising bazaars, bake sales, auctions, teas, turkey suppers. What if over-worked volunteers had more time to live out their compassionate instincts? What if even a fraction of the work directed at maintaining our properties was directed towards preaching the good news, healing broken hearts, liberating the oppressed, and opening doors to the bruised? (See Luke 4:18.)

The Distortion of Evangelism

In North America, this myopic preoccupation with church growth has distorted and damaged the Christian idea of evangelism. In most circles, evangelism is equated with recruitment— fostering healthy church membership, enhancing discipleship. In the Madison Avenue hybrid form, Christian evangelism focuses on growth, on making the church a bigger and better enterprise.

Having constructed huge sanctuaries, our gospel message is influenced by the need to maintain such large buildings, rather than save souls. We turn our efforts quite naturally and honestly in that direction. In theological terms, we have tied evangelism to ecclesiology.

On first glance, this seems to be a fair interpretation of the great injunction to preach the good news found in Matthew's Gospel:

And Jesus approached them and spoke these words: "All authority has been given to me in heaven and on earth. You are to go and make followers of all peoples. You are to baptize them in the name of the Father and the son and the holy spirit. Teach them to observe everything I commanded. I'll be with you day in and day out, as you'll see, so long as this world continues its course" (Matt. 28:18-20, SV).

There are some questions regarding the historicity of Matthew's evangelistic conclusion. Given that the Trinitarian formula ("in the name of the Father and the Son and the Holy Spirit") was a post-resurrection, post-ascension, and a very institutional Christian form of speech, it is doubtful that Jesus actually spoke these words. Scholarly consensus now argues that it is more than likely the message of early Christian missionaries, those who set out to take the world by storm, or who at least felt the message of Jesus was intended for a wider audience than Palestinian Jews.

The history of the proselytizing movement is quite vast, and I cannot hope to do justice to the many cruelties and nobilities it contains. Nevertheless, a few notes might help explain the current preoccupation with size as the standard by which to measure ecclesiastical success and evangelistic zeal.

Earlier in this century, Christian missionaries believed that God's word was meant to be preached to all people. My grandfather Cunningham trekked through the previously unknown canals (unknown to white Westerners, that is) of China with this sole purpose. In similar fashion, preachers journeyed through the back waters of India and across the plains of Africa in the hope of preaching the "good news" and converting a few more souls to Jesus. That's evangelism. The reigning slogan among many well-meaning Christians missionaries on this continent was: "The world for Christ in this century." In this spirit, church leaders dubbed the twentieth as the "Christian" century, an extravagant claim when viewed from near the close of this particularly violent hundred years.

There were clearly differing degrees of motivation for such evangelistic efforts. For instance, the dispensationalists argued

GOD HATES RELIGION

that the simple preaching of the word was sufficient. Their particular perception of Christian faith argues that the world is passing through the sixth age or dispensation—the time immediately preceding the great time of destruction. Time, for dispensationalists, was very short. Jesus was returning for the elect very soon. Consequently, grandfather in his early ministry passed out tracts that outlined the coming "dispensation" of tribulation. Having received the "Word," strangers to God's word could decide for themselves. Mainline denominations oriented their evangelism to longer-term projects, preferring to establish schools, seminaries, and local church communities. It was my grandmother, a Canadian Methodist missionary sponsored by the Women's Missionary Society, who embodied this style of evangelism in my family. The hospital compound and the Christian school were her tools and the means to build up the community of faith.

Whether conservative or liberal, the initial dream was identical. Christians wanted an ever-growing, ever-expanding body of Christ. It was intended to be numerically large, giving glory to God, embodying Christ's message. The entire world would be baptized in His name.

Later in this century, the appeal of this great dream diminished. But evangelistic enterprise is far from dead. Among North Americans, particularly those of the right, zeal for converting unbelievers is high. Evangelism, meaning increasing the numbers in the pews, reigns unchecked as a largely unquestioned Christian doctrine. Even among liberals, there has been no serious attempt to redefine evangelism. We have simply abandoned it as an outdated model of Christian witness.

Is it possible that we have been mistaken about the meaning of evangelism, of spreading the good news about Jesus? Have we been misguided when, in our zeal, we envisioned the church's mission through increasingly grandiose schemes of self-aggrandizement? The Gospels may be pointing to an alternate vision, one in which an ever-growing company of followers is specifically *not* intended. Let us imagine, if we can, a Jesus

THE SUBVERSIVE MINORITY MOVEMENT

community that never gains majority status, in which the question of increasing size is irrelevant.

The Small Community

While the parable of the leaven in the lump of dough is found in several Gospels, I turn to Matthew's version for evidence that the coming reign of God was intended to be a minority movement:

> He told them another parable: Heaven's imperial rule is like leaven that a woman took and concealed in fifty pounds of flour until it was all leavened (Matt. 13:33, SV).

Notice that in Christ's perspective of God's reign, there is no mention of the company of disciples or of a Holy Catholic Church or even of a scattered band of sympathizers. The carpenter from Galilee rarely mentions the organizational structure he expects to develop from his words (that should be a sobering thought for any evangelist). Instead, he speaks of the coming rule of God, a time when the earth will be under God's sway. Logically, the disciples perceive themselves to be the agents of that coming rule and its most immediate proponents. They picture themselves as joint rulers with Jesus, sitting in places of honour, governing great assemblies.

It is quite striking that Jesus uses images that are decidedly unimperial and unmajestic. They are non-hierarchical and largely freed from imperial implications. In his parables and sayings, there is no equation between size and God's favour and not even a hint of the idea of providential progress. On the contrary, according to Jesus, God's imperial rule appears to be a small minority movement. Like yeast in a lump of bread, its role is not to take over or to reproduce itself until its boundaries are equal to those of the society at large, turning everything into yeast. Rather, it is an enlivening agent, a proactive catalyst.

The same message is given when Jesus employs the image of

GOD HATES RELIGION

salt: "You are the salt of the earth" (Matt. 5:13, SV). Salt? What did Jesus mean? In our day, salt is the great blood pressure culprit, the slayer of many a weak heart. While we hesitate before we use it liberally, it was not so long ago that salt had a much higher reputation and was a substance revered and treasured by many. Such was its importance that Jesus even used it to describe his listeners; those who gathered to hear his Sermon on the Mount were called "the salt of the earth." We can well understand that they would accept that title with pride. Jesus was identifying his followers and friends with a very precious commodity, one that had many valuable qualities.

Salt was the universal spice, giving zing and zest to all manner of foods. Have you ever made bread without it? It is tasteless! Besides sharpening the flavour of food, salt was the great preservative, the first-century version of a deep freeze. There was no other way to keep meat or fish than to dry it and salt it. Salt was also used to comfort and heal. Even in the time of Jesus, salt springs were popular as a source of relief from the aches and pains of ageing. In addition to its soothing qualities, salt was used for the cleansing of wounds—the great healing spice. It was also used as a corrosive agent, a strange white powder that killed contagion and warded off evil spirits. Finally, salt had a mystical quality. It was the stuff of cultic sacrifices used in the temple at Jerusalem.

In this image, "salt of the earth," we encounter Jesus as the master story-teller, for who isn't moved by the richness of this label? In an age when salt was more precious than in our own, Jesus is saying to the people around him, "You are the very heart of life on this planet and central to its functioning, essential to its survival. You are magical and, yes, miraculous."

In extending the importance and foundational nature of salt to the entire Christian enterprise, our tradition has too often argued that our faith in the Lord Jesus Christ is equally important to all of life. Everyone and everything needs or benefits from salt; therefore, everyone needs and could benefit from Christian teaching. Hence, the missionary zeal of the Jesus movement and our understanding of evangelism. There's no time to lose: let's go out and baptize everyone into the "Church of the Salt of the Earth. "

In consequence, Christians have often presented themselves as the Essential Truth, the sole Guiding Light. We have committed most of our energy to converting others to that view. We have said to ourselves that we are so important, our message of "salt of the earth" so central to life, that we have to share with it everyone. You don't care for salt? Well, you're going to get it whether you want it or not.

Such was our pride of status, our over-bearing sense of self-importance, and our misguided zeal for Christ that in the name of evangelism we perpetrated many evils. There was a tribe of Native people from Papua, New Guinea, who suffered because of this Christian zeal to make "salt" of everyone. When the need arose to cut down a particular type of tree upon which the community depended for its livelihood, it was common practice for the tribal leaders and clan members to gather around the tree in question. Such was their reverence for life that they would pray and dance for hours and ask the tree for forgiveness because they had to end its life. They called upon the spirit of the tree to understand. It could take days for these people to cut down a tree, so precious was its life, so sacred its existence.

Salt-of-the-earth Christians outlawed this practice. They saw it as evil, as pagan, pantheistic nonsense. However, if the Christian tradition had mustered the same reverence for life, the same respect for God's creation, we might not be facing the current ecological crisis.

It is common knowledge that the church has a dark history as a religious organization. Throughout the ages, it has made use of torture, mass murder, extortion, and slavery to spread the message of the Jesus movement; centuries of despicable behaviour, all undertaken in the name of Christian evangelism and intended to enlarge the company of people Jesus called "the salt of the earth."

But what happens if the concentration of salt in any one place

GOD HATES RELIGION

is too high? Well, I'm not a biologist, but I do have eyes. Things die. Why is the lowest body of water in the world called the Dead Sea? Because it is so saturated with salt that all marine life has been exterminated. What happened to Lot's wife when her whole being was turned into a pillar of this most precious and important spice? She died, of course. Too much salt is a killer. And if that doesn't ring alarm bells in every Christian sanctuary and fellowship hall, I don't know what will.

What Jesus is actually saying is that his followers are not meant to take over. There is no point in everyone becoming the salt of the earth for that is a deadly mixture. Jesus consistently uses images that portray his followers as few but nevertheless potent agents of change. We are mustard seeds, leaven or yeast, a small company going about two by two, little rays of candle-light, grains of salt.

Now, it is quite a tricky thing to unravel the thoughts and motives of Jesus. It is difficult enough just trying to understand what he is saying. But given the breadth of images that were available to him, and given that he constantly looked upon his followers as a minority movement, a ginger group, it is highly questionable that Jesus ever intended his disciples to be in the majority, to become normative, the status quo. We're not meant to be on top, commanding authority and compelling conformi-ty. Christendom, the model of a "Christian society," was and is a colossal mistake.

Evangelism, then, has nothing to do with numbers and filling the pew. That's a misconception, so let's stop our hand wringing over empty seats. Evangelism is about being faithful change agents, the little bit of zest that brings things to life. That's what it truly means to be the salt of the earth.

In keeping with the small, minority images, Jesus ridicules those who equate largesse with God's blessing and purpose. A glance at the parable of the barns gives adequate testimony to the gospel's suspicion of size as a measure of God's favour.

Then he told them a parable: There was a rich man whose fields

40

produced a bumper crop. "What do I do now?" he asked himself, "since I don't have any place to store my crops. I know!" he said, "I'll tear down my barns and build larger ones so I can store all my grain and my goods. Then I'll say to myself, 'You have plenty put away for years to come. Take it easy; eat, drink, and enjoy yourself.'" But God said to him, "You fool! This very night your life will be demanded back from you. All this stuff you've collected—whose will it be now?" That's the way it is with those who save up for themselves, but aren't rich where God is concerned (Luke 12:16, SV).

How does "all this stuff you've collected," which certainly encompasses large buildings and vast assets in forms other than real estate, benefit the church? Surely it is a drain on our spiritual energies, just as the bigger barns were for the man in the parable.

A Subversive Minority

In the verses prior to those containing the leaven in the lump imagery for God's imperial rule, Jesus employs an even less grandiose image. He depicts God's reign as coming like the growth a mustard seed:

He put another parable before them with these words: "Heaven's imperial rule is like a mustard seed that a man took and sowed in his field. Though it is the smallest of all seeds, yet, when it has grown up, it is the largest of garden plants, and becomes a tree, so that the birds of the sky come and roost in its branches" (Matt. 13:31-22, SV).

When examined critically, the mustard seed image poses certain problems. It is obvious from the context of the parable that Jesus wants his listeners to focus on the difference between the small size of the seed and the large size of the final plant. But a mustard plant cannot house birds. It may be an acceptable

GOD HATES RELIGION

exaggeration on the part of Jesus, but any of his listeners would have known that mustard plants don't grow that large. Whatever we might surmise, the image is not at all triumphant. There were better images available to the master story-teller if he wanted to speak of majestic endings arising from inauspicious beginnings. Why not speak of the cedars of Lebanon? They begin from a very small cone and grow to great heights. Surely, this would serve as a more fitting image of the small becoming great.

While Jesus did intend to make the point that God's reign starts small and spreads out to be a place of safety for many, there may be another reason for Christ's use of the mustard seed and/or plant analogy. It was not a pronouncement on size, as such, so much as a discourse on style. Jesus may be calling attention to the "subversive" quality of the reign of God. The mustard plant was the first-century version of the dandelion. It grew everywhere, usually where it wasn't wanted. It would have been strange, indeed, for anyone to allow it to spread unchecked. Imagine if Jesus had said, "A certain farmer went out to plant dandelions." We would view this as bizarre, and our thoughts would immediately turn to how dandelions spread and get in the way, how they are hard to kill off or uproot. Could it be that Jesus had the same qualities in mind when he likened the reign of God to the mustard seed? Like the spread of a wild weed, the reign of God pops up where it's not expected, confounding the respected order of things, disturbing the status quo, surprising and pleasing in its unexpectedness.

There are other examples that support the company of Jesus as a subversive, ginger group. Look at the disciples grinding their own corn on the Sabbath, eating and drinking with sinners and defiled persons. And by talking with women, Jesus was, if nothing else, beginning a movement that rattled the well-established order.

42

The Healthy Church: A Subversive Company

Whether as leaven in the lump, as a grain of mustard, or as salt, the images Jesus employs to describe the coming reign of God are not triumphant or majestic. They are not designed to inspire an ever-growing movement that would take over the hearts and spirits of every being on earth. On the contrary, they seem to call for a committed band of followers whose spirit, compassion, flavour, and zest will inspire the whole—a subverting minority, a band of imaginative followers who turn the world on its head by employing standards of love and justice.

As I start to accept this vocation for the church, years of regret and endless days of "shoulds" lift from my shoulders. We Christians are who we are intended to be, no matter our small numbers. Perhaps for the first time since the church and empire joined together under Constantine and became an "official religion," the disciples of Christ are free to be that small minority movement. Not distressed over its status, but boldly proclaiming the coming reign of God in which everyone has enough and there is a place for all. In the subversive minority church, evangelism means the embodiment of that coming age of God's favour and not the enlargement of church rolls. What a relief.

Chapter 3

Itinerant or Establishment Church?

Safe upon the solid rock the ugly houses stand.
Come and see my shining palace built upon the sand.
—Edna St. Vincent Mallay 1956, 127

The Church Building Shouts: "Evermore"

Step through the door of any Christian church, especially those situated in urban centres, and what do you see? Heavy oak pews bolted to the floor, a pulpit anchored to stone pillars, tall and proud ranks of organ pipes afixed to plaster walls, all giving ample testimony to the solidity of faith. Messages imbedded in timber and rock proclaim that this house of God stands forever, unshakeable and immovable.

Apart from their aura of righteousness and the grandeur of size, church buildings also exude permanence. This is not a fly-by-night operation or weekend tent meeting but blue-chip soul security built on a firm and very real foundation! Even in rural areas, we feel it. Bricks and mortar reveal and reinforce the spirit that yearns for a safe and secure resting place.

Who can doubt the priority of place within institutional religion? Annual budgets, supposedly vehicles for reflecting God's work in the world, weigh heavily in support of the maintenance of existing structures. We must ask ourselves if heating a cavernous room for once-weekly use is God's mission, if a mammoth building truly reflects the holiness of the Creator of the

ITINERANT OR ESTABLISHMENT CHURCH?

universe. Do we believe that God would choose to keep the church doors open instead of selling its assets to feed the hungry and clothe the naked? Every year, many devout Christians struggle to maintain our buildings in the face of desperate unemployment, and yet we proclaim that we are about God's justice.

Besides the building itself, most of our liturgical furnishings emanate immovability. The long pews defy any other arrangement than theatre-style ranks and the suggestion that a few be removed for more flexibility of worship calls forth the age-old need for things to remain "as they've always been." The baptismal font, a central, holy location, is quite often too heavy to move as it is made from marble or stone, in-laid into floor tiles, or fenced off by a wooden railing. It can't go on the road. Likewise the pulpit, constructed to mirror the unshakeable, divine Word of God, is solid, anchored to the rock that cannot move. A portable soap box this is not. Reading lectern, communion table, choir loft, organ—almost all the liturgical tools for Christian worship are immovable.

Much of our spiritual freight is carried by communal singing. At a glance, most Protestant hymn books bolster the message of permanence. "Rock of Ages"; "How Firm a Foundation"; "Christ is Made the Sure Foundation." Given the preponderance of foundation imagery in our spirituality, it is no wonder that we constructed enormous rock-solid edifices as mirrors of our faith in God's steadfastness.

The Need for Shelter

Surely there was more to the search for permanence than the desire to build big buildings that reflected the imagery of our hymns. We need to appreciate the central human quest that this architecture represents. Church architecture is a language, and for two thousand years its vocabulary has been skewed towards words like "establishment," "permanence," "eternal," "unchanging."

The church building reflects the life-long search for unshakeable assurance, a cry for trustworthy shelter from the storms of human existence. This need is carved into the heavy, protective roof timbers. The memorial plaques speak of the desire for a memory that does not fade, while the high altars and lofty choir stalls point to the source of our hopes. The quiet corners of the sanctuary breathe deeply: "Here you can stop and rest, find peace and lasting tranquillity."

The fleeting nature of human life, our marching unto our own ending, pushes us, frail beings that we are, to establish a secure hold on holiness, to tie it down so that it won't escape our grasp. Since life speeds by too quickly, religion, as the antidote to death, must speak of permanence and lassitude. This lesson is built right into our religion. Turning to God in our distress, the fervent heart naturally seeks assurance, a word of lasting comfort. So modern church buildings reflect the quest for establishment. The church where I recently served is a good example. Centenary Methodist Church was built to stand forever. Steel and iron are coupled with immense wood beams, a haven for the grieving and those fearful of dying. Finely carved pews, heavy and rock-like; likewise the proud and prominent pulpit and the immensely heavy communion table. These dominant pieces of furniture say to believers, "You are not alone; your life will carry on in this place long after you have gone." The exterior facade, head and shoulders over any adjacent structure, declares God's abiding presence, announcing, "Here is the sacred, the immovable house of the Lord, built literally upon the bedrock of Canada. Grave, where is your victory? Death, where is your sting?" The eternal breaks into time in this place.

Liturgical Lethargy

There is irony here: spirituality must move to stay alive and bring solace to the lost. Once the architecture has spoken its word of permanence, what is next? Yet there is so much else that feeds the soul. If the worship space is inflexible and unchanging, the spirit may eventually wither and become stale, lifeless.

When examining the spiritual direction for new liturgical acts, the tested formula is "form follows function." First, one determines the actual content of a worshipping action. What is the purpose? What is the desired goal? What is the theological meaning? Once these questions have been answered, the physical shape or form of a worship service and its materials flow naturally enough.

Unfortunately, we are often much better at picturing form, physical buildings and furniture. Spiritual imperatives are harder to grasp. Consequently, ecclesiastical buildings often reflect a reversal of the above formula, i.e., "function follows form." We build our religion around what we know: houses, special rooms, fixed addresses. Our religious cloth is cut to fit this well-established pattern. Alas, this is still true of new church development.

Why are we surprised when our worship is ponderous and clumsy? The spirit is bound by outdated and heavy forms that encumber its free flowing.

Implicit Principles of Establishment

Church establishments are not simply a result of the reversal of a liturgical principle and a lack of religious imagination. There is also an institutionalizing process operative within any religious movement that naturally seeks to posit its own necessity. If the faith is to remain, to be passed on to subsequent generations, it needs a home, an establishment. Linked with the institutional process of religion are the vested interests of priests and other church officials. Salaries and living allowances are all dependent on gathering people and their financial resources into one place.

These financial considerations are not to be taken lightly. All too often they are the only reason some church institutions remain unchanged throughout the years. If money talks in our culture, its most consistent speech to religion begins with a variation on the theme, "Play it safe." Churches are notorious for using their economic power wisely, for accumulating large

GOD HATES RELIGION

reserves and remaining trusted "establishment" institutions.

The Gospel Response

My religious memory has tunnel vision. I remember the church of my youth and imagine that the Christian community has always taken that shape or something quite similar. I assume that there has always been a place of worship. Whether it was the "house" in Capernaum, which some archaeologists believe was Peter's house, the catacombs in Rome, or the Cathedrals of France, there has always been a house of worship. Why wouldn't this be the case, given the Judean roots of Christianity? Wasn't Solomon's temple a holy of holies, the seat of the Most High? Why wouldn't Christianity pattern itself after that "established" tradition?

In spite of the evidence, ask yourself if the company of Jesus was always established. Was the Christian faith locked into a "fixed-address" religion from its very beginnings? Think for a moment about whether there were other options, alternative visions. During the brief time between the death and resurrection of Jesus and the writing of the first Gospels, there were at least a couple of viable choices competing with the geographically established church. There remain only a few hints of their existence in the gospel record. The description of the communal church, one which treated private property and real estate in a radically ascetic manner (see Acts 2:42-47; 4:32-37), is one example. The church as a circle of scholarship, one of which may have developed the elaborate scriptural support for the passion story, is another possibility. Dominic Crossan's discussion of the death of Jesus in his work *Who Killed Jesus?* explores this latter idea. He also suggests that a unique and earlier form of church may be buried in Mark 1:35-38. Crossan's thesis in *The Historic Jesus* revolves around what may be called the "brokerless" community of faith.

Mark begins his Gospel without a nativity story. The first chapter plunges us, in his typically urgent manner, directly into

48

the ministry of Jesus. The mysterious figure from Nazareth calls his followers and begins to work miracles among the people, casting out demons, healing the sick, curing fevers, and teaching with authority. Many people come to the house of Peter hoping for a miracle.

If Jesus lived in the modern era, we would expect him to build a little shrine at the back of Peter's Capernaum home, something tasteful and soothing where he could receive the penitent and cure the righteous. Then, as the financial backing grew, he would naturally build a sanctuary. Capernaum would swell with the press of pilgrims, and before you knew it, there'd be a satellite dish on the roof and a sound studio and telecommunications centre, all done with much more class and tact than current televangelists. Jesus would be on the road to becoming an attraction. *Time* magazine would feature him in their December 24th issue and travel agents would begin to put Capernaum on the Middle East tour circuit. That's what we would expect of a religious man. Jesus would stay in Capernaum, use his good name to give some permanence, something lasting to his ministry. He would become the spiritual broker.

Instead of opting for this course of action, Jesus tells Peter that it's time to move on. Imagine the surprise and consternation of the disciples: "Move on? We're just getting under way, and you want to leave it all behind and start somewhere fresh? That doesn't make any sense. Jesus, you should listen to the voice of reason and practicality."

Jesus refuses to settle down in one place. Mark justifies this bizarre action with a hint of apocalyptic urgency: "Let's go somewhere else, to the neighboring villages, so I can speak there too, since that's what I came for" (1:38, SV). The message of the coming reign of God is so pressing it has to be told. Jesus hasn't time for a growing church and other mundane religious preoccupations. That spade work will come later with Peter and the pentecostal spirit.

It is possible that Mark, albeit unwittingly, gives evidence of a distinctly different style of Christian ministry. This ministry

GOD HATES RELIGION

refuses to establish itself, does not see geographic permanence as a benefit, but rather considers all such striving for solidity to be counter-productive. Taking their model from Jesus, who clearly wished to be known as an itinerant preacher, these people of "the Way" became a pilgrim movement. In the first century, this travelling church was an alternative to the established one.

The best evidence for seeing Jesus as the itinerant, apart from the obvious historical data in the Gospels that indicates a good deal of travelling, is found in Jesus' injunctions to his followers, the so-called mission of the twelve. Found in all three Gospels, and according to Crossan the most widely attested by independent sources (Crossan 1991, 434), this bit of historical data may contain insights for re-energizing the diminished and marginalized body of Christ in the twenty-first century.

In the canonical Gospels, we find three direct references to the mission of the twelve (Matt. 10:5-15; Mark 6:8-11; Luke 9:3-5). It has been argued that the oldest version is actually contained within Luke's story of the sending out of the seventy-two missionaries (10:1-16). Since the actual content of the story varies only slightly, we will take this version as representative of the entire collection of mission stories.

After this the Lord appointed seventy-two others and sent them on ahead of him in pairs to every town and place that he himself intended to visit. He would say to them, "Although the crop is good, still there are few to harvest it. So beg the harvest boss to dispatch workers to the fields. Get going; look, I'm sending you out like lambs into a pack of wolves. Carry no purse, no knapsack, no sandals. Don't greet anyone on the road. Whenever you enter a house, first say, 'Peace to this house.' If peaceful persons live there, your peace will rest on them. But if not, it will return to you. Stay at that one house, eating and drinking whatever they provide, for workers deserve their wages. Don't move from house to house. Whenever you enter a town and they welcome you, eat whatever is set before you. Cure the sick there and tell them,

ITINERANT OR ESTABLISHMENT CHURCH?

*'God's imperial rule is closing in.' But whenever you enter a
town and they do not receive you, go out into its streets and say,
'Even the dust of your town that sticks to our feet, we wipe off
against you. But know this: God's imperial rule is closing in.' I
tell you, on that day Sodom will be better off than that town.*

*"Damn you, Chorazin! Damn you, Bethsaida! If the miracles
done in you had been done in Trye and Sidon, they would have
sat in sackcloth and ashes and changed their ways long ago. But
Tyre and Sidon will be better off at the judgment than you. And
you Capernaum, you don't think you'll be exalted to heaven, do
you? No, you'll go to Hell.*

*"Whoever hears you hears me, and whoever rejects you re-
jects me, and whoever rejects me rejects the one who sent me"*
(Luke 10:1-16, SV).

The multiple versions of this story would indicate that it is
probably not the invention of the gospel writers themselves.
They are drawing on a much older tradition. It would be difficult to determine if the words belong to the historical Jesus.
Nevertheless, given the number of times this story appears in
distinct traditions, it is possible to argue that some core of the
story may be traced back to the Galilean visionary.

On the basis of this gospel story, it is possible to imagine that
some of the earliest attempts at responding to the crucifixion/
resurrection event took the form of a two-by-two itinerant mission. It may well have been that Jesus had his followers practice
what he himself carried out, a constant travelling mission among
the towns and villages of Galilee. Certainly for the first few
decades after Easter there is evidence that some portion of the
Jesus movement followed this pattern of not establishing house
churches but preaching to the Jews of the countryside.

It may well have been that the early two-by-two missions
held to a strict code, but as time passed, the stresses and costs of
missionary travel and the shifting emphasis of the Christian
communities tended to soften the demands. In the movement
from Luke 10 to Mark 6, we can detect the subtle yet significant

GOD HATES RELIGION

movement towards establishment as institutionalized religion intruded upon the fledgling movement with a growing leniency for the circuit riders. In contrast to Luke's Spartan admonitions, Mark's version allows that the itinerant preachers can carry a staff for protection and sandals for comfort.

As the community of Jesus moved into the second century of the common era, the practice of itinerant preachers dwindled, corruption eroded its authority, and the early church was obliged to establish rules for discerning true preachers from false ones.

It is important to remember that this missionary movement appears to be distinct from that of Paul. Rather than moving into a town for the creation of a church community, which was Paul's style, these countryside missionaries were sent on a sort of "blitz" campaign. There was no thought of establishing churches. They moved on before anyone would or could begin to form a structure or community around their ministry. A close analogy would be the roving dispensationalists, who, at the turn of this century, travelled the roads and spoke in market after market for only an evening or two, getting the message out and then moving on to the next village. The urgency of the "imperial rule of God" pushed the early missionaries as it did the twentieth-century dispensationalists. There was no time for settlement.

Assuming that some form of instruction regarding the spiritual fellowship found in Luke 10 was given to either the first followers of Jesus or to the post-resurrection Galilean nucleus of believers, the question remains: What was the point? Why would Jesus or the early community of believers want to live or work under those very harsh conditions? Was it faith, naiveté, or revolutionary zeal that drove them out two by two? Travelling under any circumstance in the first century was dangerous. To refuse even the minimum protection of a staff was asking for trouble. Without a cloak or extra clothing, one risked the likely possibility of overexposure to the elements, for nights in the wilderness are very cold indeed. Having no bag for money or bread robs the traveller of any means of purchasing or carrying

52

ITINERANT OR ESTABLISHMENT CHURCH?

provisions. How would they eat? What if they found no one to take them in?

Why the severity of the mission? There are both practical and theological answers to that question. First, the practical. Jouette Bassler suggests that Jesus wished his followers to be distinguishable from the travelling Cynic philosophers who also walked the roadways as an act of devotion. Apparently Cynics (from a derogatory use of the Greek word for dog) went about the ancient world with a begging bag, relying upon the generosity of those they met. Their message, implicit in the very form of their travel, was simple: luxury was a corrosive agent, eating away at the heart of society. Wealth and real estate led to hypocrisy and ignorance, and true enlightenment could only be achieved through poverty. The point was to emphasize their disdain of material goods through radical poverty. Travelling about naked to the elements, so to speak, they hoped to spread the philosophy of richness of spirit through relinquishment of material goods.

Jesus' followers were not to resemble Cynics. Without a begging bag or knapsack, they could not beg. They were clearly not allowed to ask for food. On the contrary, they were to give without expectation of reward. Upon entering a town, they were to bestow a blessing, cure the sick, and spread the message of the coming reign of God. In a paradoxical way, hospitality for these itinerant prophets was a gift, an opportunity given to the host by the missionaries themselves. When the family meal was shared with these strangers, their fellowship was a sign that the message of God's coming reign had been understood, that it would be lived out on the spot. At this table, everyone has a place, no one is left out, and the Spirit of Christ is born again. Such a subtle understanding of the shared food was eventually lost, and the meal became known more as a wage, as something due to the messenger, than a re-enactment of the message.

It is also possible to interpret this early style of Christian discipleship as apocalyptic in origin. There was a driving urgency among the first few clusters of Christ's followers. Christ

GOD HATES RELIGION

would come back soon, and the earth was to be prepared for the coming reign of the Lord. Such an urgent message could not wait for planned expansions of religious enterprises. Sod-turning ceremonies would have been a distraction. The time was now! So imminent was Christ's return that thought was not given even for adequate provisions. This same apocalyptic spirit has driven countless believers out onto the road who "don't fret about tomorrow" (Matt. 6:34, SV).

Apart from the dispensationalists just mentioned, Franciscans and Dominicans also took up both travelling and an impoverished lifestyle in an attempt to recreate the urgency of the early Christian message.

The medium does embody a message and there are several theological reasons for the people of Jesus to be distinguished as poor and vulnerable. If Jesus sent out his followers with these scanty provisions, it is logical to assume that he wanted to establish a "trusting" missionary style. Those who first ventured out beyond his circle would have to depend upon others, relying totally on their hospitality, protection, and guidance. These disciples were called upon to live out a radical message of trust. Just as Christ called upon believers to trust in God, who, according to the sermon on the mount, feeds the hungry and clothes the sparrows (Matt. 6:26), so these missionaries were to eat and sleep by trust. The petition of the Lord's prayer, "Give us this day our daily bread," was to be quite literally the routine life of Christ's followers.

Who can fail to be inspired by such a practical application of the message? Trust, if it is real, is a lived reality. It cannot be understood in the abstract. You have to feel and breathe and touch and eat it.

In a similar fashion, the itinerant mission symbolized an egalitarian lifestyle. The disciples had no temple, no liturgical garb or community status to raise their profile above that of others. They entered towns as unknowns, without status, and shared what they had to offer—miracles and a message. In return, they received what the people had to offer, a meal and a bed. Here was the heart of Christ's teaching being lived out, the equal sharing of spiritual and material resources. Picture such a company of wild-eyed strangers knocking at doors, living out the gospel. Either worlds of suspicion and animosity would dissolve, walls of prejudice and pretence would be thrown down, or else the door would be barred shut. Such was the risk of unestablished religion.

I believe it is important to explore the original context within which this text would have been read. The radical poverty of the missionaries that seems so blatant to affluent North Americans would not have been so outstanding in their day. Of course, these followers would be viewed as penniless, but so were many people. Poverty was much more visible to the eye of the common citizen than is the case for us. Surely the most impressive aspect of these preachers' destitution would be the homelessness that their mission implied. These people were deliberately putting themselves at risk, leaving the protection of clan ties and community structures. They were effectively living beyond the comfortable confines of law and order.

What could this homelessness imply about the Jesus movement? The lack of an established home might signify two truths about the mission of Christianity. First, the church is not able to establish itself because it is travelling. Both materially and spiritually, the church is "on the way," emphasizing a theological incompleteness through its itinerancy, living without the assurance of iron-clad answers.

A second theological reason for this style of ministry is that the missionaries had no time to set themselves up as spiritualists, to function as the local wonder workers or become the centre of religious activity. There was no way for them to slip into the role of country parson, respected spiritual advisor and leader. Each dawn brought a new challenge of making the gospel alive to strangers, of depending again on the vision of an egalitarian community of believers to inspire belief. This style of spiritual communication quite clearly gives individuals the freedom of and responsibility for their own faith.

GOD HATES RELIGION

It is difficult to know the exact intention of Jesus, but linked with other texts, such as the sermon on the mount (Matt. 5ff) and the series of gospel sayings about believers being like foxes without holes and birds without nests (Luke 8:58), a composite picture begins to emerge. Christ may never have intended his movement to become established. It is possible that he envisioned a constant revolutionizing itinerancy as the *modus operendi* of his followers. Could this not be a lost tradition, one of the early experiments in Christian evangelism, a gap in the seemingly seamless fabric of the Christian institutionalization of belief?

Whatever the original intent, the established church moved quickly to close the gap, to organize and regulate the itinerants, and eventually to localize and domesticate asceticism. It was not long before religious authorities warned of "false" preachers and began to establish bishops and deacons, house churches and seminaries.

As Crossan argues, the time when the world could be changed by the knock of a wandering radical had passed.

A Church without Walls

On the basis of these gospel texts, I agree with the current critics of religion who argue that the ponderous weight of ecclesiastical real estate is a colossal misunderstanding or misinterpretation of the initial mission of Jesus. "The rock" upon which the master said he would build a church has been taken quite literally. "Church" means solid foundations and immovable walls. In contrast, I believe the Galilean peasant prophet intended his followers to be marked by a radically "light" itinerancy, by an unwillingness to lay claim to any spiritual or material territory. It was their faith in a no-fixed-address approach to God that was rock solid. Jesus wanted a mission where all stood on equal footing, with the missionary imparting a miracle or healing and the hosts sharing a meal and the blessing of security.

We are faced again with the problem of historicity. Is the

ITINERANT OR ESTABLISHMENT CHURCH?

original, historical intent of the Jesus movement, so far as we can determine, to be normative for all ages? This has certainly been the assumption up to now. Almost all the reform movements of Christianity have attempted to recapture the original simplicity (Mennonite), poverty (Franciscan), or anti-clerical (Anabaptist) community of that early period.

Few of these reforms have endured. Perhaps this is to their credit, since I believe the original idea of Jesus at Nazareth was not to establish a new "Jesus" cult so much as to disestablish the unhelpful approach to faith institutionalized in the religion of his day.

Our predicament, one named in prior chapters, is to transcreate the basic tenets of that gospel message into today's context. What does a first-century itinerant, egalitarian mission look like in late twentieth-century garb? In a very obvious form it means getting out of real estate or using our physical plants in radically different ways. We may decide to risk our trust funds for the sake of the gospel, not worrying about whether the church will survive into the next century but concentrating on being faithful here and now.

The vision of an itinerant community of faith may well mean an adjustment of our church goals and objectives, removing the assumptions of permanence and replacing them with visions of imminence and itinerancy. Perhaps we should design our worship, education, and service to go on the road, living with the people who need healing as those first preachers did. In modern parlance, we would cease being a passive institution and become pro-active. It may be that the time has come to rejuvenate the spiritual pilgrimage, the physical journey that embodies the movement of the soul. Is this not a faithful response to the gospel's story of going out on the road?

Finally this early vision of the itinerant church implies a mission of justice, an egalitarian message implicit within its structure. The early two-by-two mission, if it is lived today, means equality for all people according to their needs. Everyone has a vital gift to offer and none need fear rejection. In this itinerant

GOD HATES RELIGION

church, the resources are not wasted on buildings, but reserved for those we meet on the journey—the lost and wounded.

Chapter 4

The Church:
Centrifugal or Centripetal Force?

When, therefore, John the Baptist with a magical rite or Jesus with a magical touch cured people of their sickness, they implicitly declared their sins forgiven or nonexistent. They challenged not the medical monopoly of the doctors, but the religious monopoly of the priests. All of this was religiopolitically subversive.

—Crossan 1991, 324

"Can I Get My Baby Done?"

The phone rings, and a tentative voice asks, "Can I get my baby done?" What sounds like a request for a plumbing job or an electronic adjustment is, in the caller's mind, a query regarding a necessary religious act—baptism. Without waiting for my reply, the floodgates open. "Is it all right if my husband takes pictures? Of the baptism, I mean? It's about time, don't you think? You see, my boy is ten months old and you don't want him to go much longer, do you?"

Although outwardly helpful, my inward religious sensibilities are being rubbed against the grain. "There is a special Sunday set aside for baptisms, and we would be pleased..."

"Special Sunday? Well, there's a family reunion coming up next week, and I thought it would be nice if you could do him while everyone is back home. I ... ah ... don't want anything to

59

GOD HATES RELIGION

happen to him, and while he's such a good boy, I thought you might put everything right with him now, before he's too old. You know ... bless him."

In ministerial circles, baptism stories are the stuff of standard jokes that make light of those who want their kids "done." I am often inclined to scoff at such requests, to admonish the un-thinking inquirer with a weighty theological tongue-lashing: "Baptism is a sacred sacrament. It isn't 'done' to anyone." But as I listen to that snobbish voice of mine within, the situation becomes clearer. It's not their misunderstanding of the baptis-mal act, bordering on superstition, that I lament. Rather, I am dismayed by the barriers of "official" religion, the ponderous doctrinal principles that hinder God's blessing of new life. There are invisible signs around the baptismal font that read "Danger. No trespassing."

Here a stranger is calling me, the "priest," the "holy man," the "magician," and asking me to "bless" her child. Why me? I wasn't present through the worries and doubts of pregnancy. I didn't give birth to this new life or see it well into the world. I can't touch the nagging doubt that mingles with joy as a sepa-rate being breaks off from a wholeness that lasted nine months. Why, then, am I the one to put things right, to "do" her baby? She has already blessed him, made him sacrosanct and whole according to the Creator's design. Could she not "do" him herself?

Religion answers "no." She can't "do" her baby because she has not been invested with the power, the authority, the spiritu-al strength, the magic, whatever you want to call it. She needs someone else's help, my authoritative hand. It is not surprising that in a traditionally patriarchal religion, this outside authority rests most often with men. This mother needs a patron, a spirit-ual broker to act on her behalf.

The principle of patronage, even in this "free" world, is so commonplace as to be invisible. Outside of the religious sphere, people seek patrons without a second thought. If you want to find a job, everybody knows that you have to know "somebody." If you want to obtain a good parking spot at the lot around the corner from your office, you have to have "contacts." If you are looking for a good deal in real estate, in the purchase of a car, you have to get "on the inside track." All these euphemisms mask the rather harsh and often unjust reality of patronage.

In our society, major political decisions, commercial deals, and philanthropic bequests are made on the basis of a complex network of interlocking friendships, unwritten favours, and commonly accepted self-interest. Virtue, principle, and value are the window dressings of patronage.

In our society, where "all persons are made equal," we still assume that we will need more influence than brains or luck if we are going to get ahead. In every walk of life, there are power brokers who can make or break the careers of the aspiring. Without thinking, we who are mere mortals line up at the doors of these giants, hoping to ingratiate ourselves and win favour, perhaps even aspiring eventually to turn the tables and establish ourselves as "king pins" in the game of patronage.

Patronage is a tired old shoe, is it not? Far from being the mere illegitimate underbelly of a liberated, democratic culture, influence peddling has a very colourful and ancient history. Prior to the emergence of the notion of individual freedom, patronage was even more firmly entrenched as a way of life. Highly stratified societies gave careful attention to patronly order, with each level acting as the broker for those below.

The Hebraic community of Jesus was no exception. (See Crossan's texts for a scholarly explanation of this theme in most Mediterranean cultures.) Despite the poverty of many, there was a well-established pecking order built on the assumptions of patronage. In all matters of life, one needed a patron. From the King to the lowest Galilean peasant, everyone expected, even preferred, to attract the attention and assistance of a patron. In turn, one looked to establish oneself as patron over others.

As a result, important business, whether political, economic,

GOD HATES RELIGION

or religious in nature, was not conducted in a direct, face-to-face manner. One used contacts, sought audiences through the good graces of a patron, borrowed another's good reputation, and employed letters of introduction. Modern conveniences such as the telephone, fax machine, and modem have created a culture of immediate access, but in the ancient world, there was no direct route to the emperor, to the landed aristocrat, or to God. The supplicant needed a go-between.

Now, lay aside this book for a moment and read the twenty-third chapter of Matthew's Gospel. Is it not a rather harsh condemnation of religious hierarchy? Ask yourself if it is possible that Jesus is condemning the brokering of religion, if he is casting doubts on the monopoly of spiritual leadership.

The biblical text of the Acts of the Apostles gives testimony to a "communal" church that tried to live out the unbrokered life of faith. There may have been other similar experiments. Nevertheless, given human nature, it was inevitable that we should impute to our faith systems the same patterns that operate in our secular organizations. As the Christian faith grew into an "establishment," the priests and rulers of the local institution gained their own prominence as earthly patrons, as keys to the vaults of divine favour.

The View from the Back of the Church

No matter how much we protest to the contrary, this structure of patronage still exists. The pastor or priest continues to be set on a pedestal, honoured as the focal point of worship, respected as the broker for spiritual affairs.

Let us take off our Christian spectacles and look at this building from the back of the sanctuary as if for the first time. What is most striking? What is our worship space saying above all else? Are the seats all facing in one direction? Are they oriented toward a particular object or piece of furniture? Who will be the centre of attention when the service begins? Who holds the power of speech in having the microphone? Where is the brass

62

and ornate woodwork found and who touches it?

It is obvious that one person is in charge. This is an performer-audience arena, a repetition of the ancient pattern of cult sacrifice. There is a holy of holies, the altar or table. There is a priestly caste protected by spiritual boundaries. There is a space for those who must use the offices of the officiant in order to touch the transcendent. Most churches say, "This is a place of spiritual brokerage."

This pattern has been partially undermined in the Protestant church through the burgeoning influence of lay persons. A liturgical renaissance that accentuates congregational participation has given the laity more importance, and a similar movement is evident in the post-Vatican II Roman Catholic communion. Nevertheless, the clerical priority in worship has not been substantially altered. Our services are still centred around a well-orchestrated pattern of words and gestures, performed by a central priest or minister who has the sole privilege of presiding over sacraments.

The principle of mediation is also found in the practice of many prayers. Theological paradigms have ranked the order of supplications. In descending order, we have God the Creator, Jesus the Son, Holy Spirit, Mary the mother of Jesus and the disciples, a heavenly host of well-attested saints, and finally a host of witnesses, local personalities who have gone before us. All of these levels of patronage are used to relay our petitions upward, through the many heavenly layers, to God. Even where there is no mediator between God and the human soul, as in the most adamant Protestant denominations, we punctuate our prayers with an obvious brokerage formula: "We ask these things in the name of Jesus Christ our Lord." Our faith is transmitted through an intermediary. Priests and ministers are Christ's representatives on earth, serving as the medium through which spiritual messages are passed between Christ and the community of faith. Ergo, the question of baptism and the request from the woman that I "do" her baby.

The traditionalists may ask, Is the structure of patronage a

GOD HATES RELIGION

problem? Why should we be distressed if the church patterns itself after a time-tested and quite natural principle? Are there really any difficulties with brokered spirituality? They argue that some believers cannot worship except through the assistance of a mediator. They require the minister or priest to act as religious broker, the gifted one who can speak well and true. They argue that this leader or functionary has the training and skill to discern the spirit of the people, to channel their sentiments and, through experience, aid the devout to touch the divine in a fashion impossible for the untrained lay person.

While there is merit in a trained and wise ecclesiastical leadership, we would be naive if we ignored how the structure of the medium shapes the message.

Does Religion Have a Centrifugal or Centripetal Force?

When the spiritual message passes through the hierarchical screen of ecclesiastical patronage, it is distorted and weakened. Like a centripetal force, priest-centred religion concentrates power in the hands of a few. While this may assist in the maintenance of order, it also disempowers ordinary folk who believe they have no direct access to God. An important distinction is made when lay people are distanced from their Creator by architecture and liturgical practice. The mediated experience of God, being of lesser degree and inferior to that of the priest, is a reflection of one's unacceptability. How quickly the equation is made: religious presiders are good since they are closer to God, while rejects and sinners are quite naturally weeded out as they stand further from the holy place. Shuffling their feet in the narthex, waiting for their turn to approach the high table, the lay persons, doubters, marginalized, weak, and lost are shamed and further diminished by the system of religious patronage.

The question arises (one that sparked the Protestant Reformation): Is there an "authentic" approach to spiritual enlightenment that is not mediated? Is the priest-centred pattern of holiness the only route to the divine? While leadership is impor-

64

tant, worship and spiritual enlightenment are directed by the community of faith. It is this gathered company who are approaching God and, in many instances, they have no need of a broker. If disciples feel closer to God in a natural setting, on a walk or during work, this pattern of devotion should be identified and honoured as valid communion with the Creator.

The chief question is whether the people are empowered by their patterns of spiritual devotion. In the Hebrew Scriptures, God repeatedly asks the people of Israel what happens to the ones who have no power or status. How are they treated? This yardstick of justice should be the measure of our spiritual enlightenment. How restricted are the homeless, the poor, the lonely and broken-hearted, the doubters? Do they have equal or even preferred access to the tools of spiritual strength in our communities?

At the heart of the Judeo-Christian tradition is a principle that governs most world religions. For lack of better words, I will employ the phrase coined by Paul Tillich and call it the "protestant principle." Essentially, this principle argues that transcendence, the spirit of the divine, is non-negotiable. There is nothing that the believer can do to deserve, earn, or merit communion with the eternal. It is essentially a gift. If this principle governs Christian faith, there is no real need for a priesthood. Within worship, someone must act as a guiding presence, giving people the courage or wisdom to accept what is given to all. But ministers, priests, or pastors do not have a corner on the divine, nor do they wield a unique right to convey special indulgences or confer merit. The spiritual gifts of God are not bound by any human distinctions. At the very heart of faith, the believer stands alone before God, and the communion is direct, unbrokered, unmediated. This was evident to Jesus even in his time, for he came to break the monopoly of the priests and religious rulers of his day.

GOD HATES RELIGION

The Choice

If you feel inclined towards the protestant principle, to seeing religion as an unmediated experience, to distrust of the hierarchical patterns of established religion, you will be encouraged to know that the gospel agrees with you. It contains many accounts of Jesus confronting the brokerage of the religious rulers. One of the most confounding and revolutionary aspects of his ministry may have been his refusal to play the patronage game.

There is no better example of Jesus' refusal to act as spiritual patron than the story of the meal at the house of Simon, the Pharisee. Found in the Gospel of Luke, it is one representation of a wider tradition involving an unnamed woman and the anointing of Jesus. (See also Matt. 26:6-13, Mark 14:3-9, and John 12:1-8.)

> One of the Pharisees invited him to dinner; he entered the Pharisee's house, and reclined at the table. A local woman, who was a sinner, found out that he was having dinner at the Pharisee's house. She suddenly showed up with an alabaster jar of myrrh, and stood there behind him weeping at his feet. Her tears wet his feet, and she wiped them dry with her hair; she kissed his feet, and anointed them with the myrrh.
>
> The Pharisee who had invited him saw this and said to himself, "If this man were a prophet, he would know who this is and what kind of woman is touching him, since she is a sinner."
>
> And Jesus answered him, "Simon, I have something to tell you."
>
> "Teacher," he said, "speak up."
>
> "This moneylender had two debtors; one owed five hundred silver coins, and the other fifty. Since neither one of them could pay, he wrote off both debts. Now which of them will love him more?"
>
> Simon answered, "I would imagine, the one for whom he wrote off the larger debt."
>
> And he said to him, "You're right." Then turning to the

woman, he said to Simon, "Do you see this woman? I walked into your house and you didn't offer me water for my feet; yet she has washed my feet with her tears and dried them with her hair. You didn't offer me a kiss, but she hasn't stopped kissing my feet since I arrived. You didn't anoint my head with oil, but she has anointed my feet with myrrh. For this reason, I tell you, her sins, many as they are, have been forgiven, as this outpouring of her love shows. But the one who is forgiven little shows little love."

And he said to her, "Your sins have been forgiven."

Then those having dinner with him began to mutter to themselves, "Who is this who even forgives sins?"

And he said to the woman, "Your trust has saved you; go in peace" (Luke 7:36-50, SV).

To comprehend how this passage of Scripture addresses the question of spiritual brokerage and ecclesiastical hierarchy, it is necessary to highlight those points that would be sensitive to a Semitic ear and which are mostly lost to the North American worldview.

Let us first ask what the underlying cultural messages are in this text. Jesus is invited for dinner at the home of a Pharisee. As I stated in chapter 1, a Pharisee was a "good" and well-respected person. Sharing a meal was a meaningful gesture, both in the offering and in the acceptance. So Luke sets the stage: This is not an idle conversation or chance meeting. This is a meal and that means intimacy and communion. Simon the Pharisee is declaring that Jesus is a suitable companion, pure enough and orthodox enough in his keeping of the law that he may dip his bread in a common dish with the Pharisee. Jesus acknowledges this religious man's worthiness, showing, if not his approval, certainly his willingness to be associated with Simon.

It is difficult to make safe assumptions about customs associated with eating in a culture so distant from our own. Local practices and anomalies play havoc with what are considered to be accurate historical traditions. Nevertheless, the text seems to assume that Jesus is reclined for his meal, with his legs stretched

GOD HATES RELIGION

away from the food, when the woman enters the room and begins anointing his feet.

The gospel story states, albeit in coded language, that this is no ordinary woman. She is "a sinner." More than likely this phrasing refers to some sexual impropriety, adultery perhaps, but most likely prostitution. The mention of an alabaster jar fits the picture of a woman of the night. It has been suggested that it was a symbol or advertizing tool for prostitutes. Small enough to be worn between the breasts, the jar with its fragrant aroma functioned both as an enticement and a deodorant. What an interesting symbol the jar becomes. A discredited woman comes into the presence of the religious authorities of her community and, in emptying the alabaster jar, proclaims an end to her defiling trade. Is an act of penance, repentance, or conversion hidden here?

No matter the intention of the anointing, this sinner would not have been welcome in the company of men and certainly not in the household of a Pharisee. Quite apart from the clear impropriety of a woman interrupting an entirely male company, this woman's impurity was contagious. A meal was a particularly sensitive time and place for such defilement. For instance, women who were menstruating or who were touching other bodily fluids were banned from the community because of their contaminating power.

We might transcreate the intent of Luke's tale in this way. Here is a toxic substance, a virus-coughing street woman who is the victim of tuberculosis, entering an AIDS isolation unit. What a dramatic scene. The tension in the story is so thick you can almost touch it.

The more I reflect on this story, the more I squirm. Jesus, a malcontent and rabble-rouser, finds himself in the home of the established authority. He's hit the big time. Most of us would be minding our manners, trying not to appear too foolish. Then, with the appearance of this woman, everything starts to unravel. Not only is she a woman, not only is she a prostitute, but she's obviously sufficiently acquainted with Jesus to perform

THE CHURCH: CENTRIFUGAL OR CENTRIPETAL FORCE?

the personal service of anointing his feet. Simon and, by extension, all his other guests are shocked.

Imagine the excitement of the first crowd to hear this story, possibly a peasant community. As with a Shakespearean comedy, the people who think they are "good" are faced with the honesty and virtue of those they believe are "bad." Social etiquette is turned on its head in a delicious reversal of roles. No doubt there was quite a stir among the original listeners.

The story continues: Simon is upset, and Jesus responds to his obvious consternation with a parable. Two men are debtors, one for a great amount, the other, for a smaller sum. If they are forgiven their debts, who will be the more loving? The Pharisee answers correctly that the one who owes much will love more when the greater debt is forgiven. It is also quite possible to apply the parable to the Pharisee's need for forgiveness. Perhaps we are to understand that it is the Pharisee who owes much, and the moralism is intended to be an ironic twist, heard by the listeners and missed by the Pharisee.

At this point, Jesus takes the radical step of making everyone in the room pay attention to the woman. He focuses the debate on someone they consider to be beneath recognition; disconcerting for the company, to say the least. Then Jesus begins to question the hospitality of the host, a dubious and embarrassing act in our culture, but an unthinkable, grievous insult in a world built on the firm foundation of honour. And then, to add insult to social injury, he employs vulgar language by referring to his feet, a part of the body never mentioned in polite company. Jesus risks alienating all the "righteous" people when he takes the side of a questionable intruder.

There is a choice embedded in this story, for Luke is not a detached philosopher; he wants to put us on the spot. Either Jesus is a great leader, one who lives above social norms and beyond the considerations of etiquette, or he is a social boor, a very troublesome and troubled misfit. How will we choose? For the choices go beyond the person of Jesus. We are asked to judge between a "righteous" spiritual path, one governed by rules and

GOD HATES RELIGION

strict regulations regarding purity, and a way of believing structured on forgiveness and a transcendent graciousness that inspires great love and devotion. Which will we choose?

In this passage, I can begin to glimpse the vision of a unique religious company that binds all the lost and rejected ones, a community in which spiritual gifts are not guarded by walls of doctrine and bound by ropes of polity. Here is a church where the blessings of God are given to all according to their gifts.

Rather than placing the spiritual power of forgiveness in the hands of a few "good" people or in a complex system of rules controlled by the intellectual elite, this Jesus liberates people to live by the love they have received from God. Pay attention to the wording of this passage from Luke. It is not a human pronouncement that brings wholeness to this woman. The love of God, which appears as great forgiveness, engenders her faith. It is God's prior love that brings liberation, not the words or actions of a priest.

Which system of spiritual enlightenment will we choose? Of course, Luke would have us choose the "Lord's way," a discipleship in which God is present to all—no earthly patrons, no mediators. The Third Gospel's weight is always pushing to the margins, undermining the human desire to concentrate spiritual power in the hands of a few righteous people.

The Pomp and Power of a Centripetal Religion

This centrifugal message of the gospel is evident in most instances where Jesus confronts the powers and principalities of Judean religion. In the Gospel of Mark, we have an example of a direct attack on the religious leaders and their oppressive monopolization of religion.

> *During the course of his teaching he would say: "Look out for the scholars who like to parade around in long robes, and insist on being addressed properly in the marketplaces, and prefer important seats in the synagogues and the best couches at banquets.*

THE CHURCH: CENTRIFUGAL OR CENTRIPETAL FORCE?

They are the ones who prey on widows and their families, and recite long prayers just to put on airs. These people will get a stiff sentence!" (Mark 12:38-39, SV).

Here, Jesus warns his listeners against a centripetal religion, against those who would commandeer religious power for their own advancement. He is set against those who control the spiritual mechanisms so that they reflect well on their own persons while dispossessing the powerless and vulnerable. Christ's judgement is severe, not only because of the pretence and foolishness of the priestly caste, but because they have injured others through their pomp and kept the fruits of God's grace from enriching many ordinary people. According to Jesus, the religious authorities have turned spirituality into a show, focusing on external matters for the sake of their own advancement.

The anti-clerical, anti-monopolist view of the gospel and Christ's ministry has inspired many reforms within the church. The Zwinglian, Lutheran, and Wesleyan Reformations are but a few examples. The message of God's grace quite naturally breaks through the presumption of possession. It is a centrifugal force pushing out to the edges, resting most comfortably when it is shared beyond the limits of the community of faith. Of course, there are many political implications to a centrifugal religion. It does not blend well with temporal, hierarchical authorities, since it spreads its authority among many and there is no one ruler or spokesperson who can be bought or controlled by political rulers. It also tends to be a more volatile and unruly religion. It should not surprise us that only the more centripetal, priest-controlled versions of faith have been "recognized" by the emperors and presidents of the secular world.

The vehement attack on small grassroots communities in Latin America is a case in point. These "churches" are largely mistrusted by dictatorships and military governments because they are diffuse, uncontrollable, prone to making decisions on their own, and do not rigidly adhere to the rules of the higher

GOD HATES RELIGION

religious authorities. The powers and principalities know, often better than believers themselves, that the gospel message is subversive precisely because it seeks to include everyone in God's reign.

The Church: An Unbroken Circle

Institutions can sin as much as individuals. It would not be an exaggeration to suggest that the recurring corporate sin of the church has been its creeping centripetal bias. It may be the dynamic of human communities in general or the particular penchant of a religious body, but we are continually struggling against the undue control of the "keys to salvation." It is not appropriate for the gifts of liberation or salvation to be in the hands of a few, until recently, exclusively male priests and ministers.

Imagine what our churches would become if the monopoly of spiritual brokers was seriously questioned. Communities of faith would naturally designate one of their own members as having "authority" over certain spiritual matters. How often, at least in the churches where I have worshipped, has this person been acknowledged by all? Leaders come and go, but that special grandmother figure, or the quiet wise elder, has the trust of the church family. Surely they should be given the responsibility for pronouncing God's blessing and sharing God's gifts, for spreading these spiritual gifts throughout the community. When that happens, we will become an unbroken circle with no place of prominence reserved for a spiritual patron. Congregations would not need to focus on the priests' actions or the minister's gestures. Religious gatherings would become more communal, participatory, and inviting.

There is a new church coming, one in which the central movement will be centrifugal. Searching and serious members of this community of faith will not tolerate an exclusivist or elitist approach to faith. In this new gathering, the question of baptism may be less troubling as it will be an option for all who desire it. It may be offered as a rite performed by the midwife or the mother herself at the time of birth. Of course, as this company of Jesus departs from the hierarchical models of religion, it will no longer carry the cultural "stamp of approval." Consequently, fewer and fewer outsiders will seek it out for the sake of fulfilling a cultural expectation. At that point, this restructured Christian church may be liberated and able to serve God and society more faithfully.

Chapter 5

Sin as a State of Being

"Spirit!... hear me! I am not the man I was. I will not be the man I must have been but for this intercourse. Why show me this, if I am past all hope?... Assure me that I yet may change these shadows you have shown me, by an altered life."

—Dickens 1972, 52-53

The "Surpriselessness" of Religion

"I be two! I be two!" That's what little Maude shouts as she waltzes around the dining room on her second birthday. Her smile whirls by as she waves her arms in all directions. She's caught up in a moment of ecstasy. What a wonderful surprise for her, a day of exaltation. Yesterday, a regular fall day in October, she was only one (a lowly and insignificant age when viewed from the dizzying heights of advanced toddlerhood), and today she is two, a mature and proper age, one of which to be proud. And it all happened without any effort; you just wait long enough, and bingo—you're one year older.

In this one instant of joy, all else is blotted out. Ask Maude if she notices the wind blowing the beautiful fall leaves off the trees. Is she wringing her hands, worrying about the growing national debt? Ask her if she is even aware that the Monster Trucks show is coming to the local arena. Not even the odd snowflake in the chill morning air can turn her mind from the sheer joy of this day. I be two! Her surprise triumphs over all else.

SIN AS A STATE OF BEING

Do you wonder what has happened to wonder, to the "strange warming of the heart" (in Wesley's words), to the surprise of the Spirit? Can we who have attended church, lo these many years, recall the last time we felt the heart-stopping, mind-fogging exhilaration of a child? Have we lost it? In our earnest desire to grow up and become responsible adults, have we mislaid the capacity to be surprised by life, by the gifts God has bestowed on us?

What a shame, an unforgivable sin, that life holds so few surprises any more. Look adulthood squarely in the face and ask yourself if it is all you hoped it would be. We struggle out of bed in the morning, groan our way through breakfast. Then into the car, hands grasped tightly on the wheel, trying to clear the mist from our eyes. Who has time to stop and be surprised? We have to get to work. Once at our desk or shop floor, there are forms to fill out, messages to return, orders to fill. Busy and boring; such is our lifestyle. After we hit thirty, we imagine that this is the way it must and should be. Built into the North American lifestyle is the belief that there are no hidden treasures buried beneath our daily routine; no "Ah, ha!" moments awaiting us at the next coffee break—just drudgery. Get up, work, eat, sleep.

"Life is empty." Is that the epitaph we should hang over the latter part of the twentieth century? As adults, we have settled into a comfortable, emotional coma, no longer able to feel surprise over laughter-filled events or moments of triumph. "Happy Birthday to You" is a perfunctory jingle, not a heartfelt wish and certainly not an expectation. As we are unmoved by joy, so we are also desensitized to evil, no longer feeling anything in response to the mass slaughter in Auschwitz, Hiroshima, Mi Lai, Chile, Guatemala, South Africa, Bosnia, Rwanda. No response to the death of a single small child, abducted and lost to view. In our cultivated cynicism, we mumble, "There's nothing new under the sun."

When I enter a church and look at the well-ordered pews, an inner voice cries out, "Will all our surprise be stifled and all our

75

GOD HATES RELIGION

joy strangled? Will our worship of the Creator of the universe become as routine and uninspiring as brushing our hair?" Alas, how often does organized religion, fearing the disorder and incipient chaos of the expressive and ecstatic Spirit of God, regulate the religious response and curb our imagination, placing blinkers on the outpouring of our compassion? We willingly become blind to the surprising Spirit of God when it comes dressed in unexpected garb.

Listen carefully to the voices of those who no longer attend our worship. They have not left because we are too harsh and demanding. People stay away in droves because we are too predictable and too joyless. There is a hunger in our culture for the substance and wonder of the spirit. This hunger the institutional church has steadfastly refused to feed, thinking that faith should not smile or laugh or play. That would be "sugar coating" the tradition.

As we stand in the midst of the sanctuary, what do we see? It is the order of worship that is most obvious. What we see in this place is expected and well orchestrated; it is not a location for great events of the heart, but for well-tuned performances.

Who would come here searching for the novel tug of the soul, the supple stirring of the Spirit? Not a whisper is heard. The unwritten message handed out by too many churches along with their bulletins is, "We'll have nothing surprising, if you please." There's no breathing space for inspiration, no spiritual room to manoeuvre. We're not expecting the unexpected; we're not open for surprises. Architectural intransigence reflects a deeper and more serious problem. There is an unspoken abhorrence of the different, a fear that is often fixated on the "stranger."

It is possible that people don't darken the door of our churches because they do not feel welcome. If they look out of the ordinary, if they do not fit into the middle-class norm, they may find themselves ignored or marginalized. These outsiders to the religious club perceive, perhaps better than the insiders themselves, that church-goers have a very low tolerance for the exceptional. If the men wear ponytails and the women wild

76

SIN AS A STATE OF BEING

dresses, what will happen? If these visitors to the church belong to a motorcycle gang or are gay or lesbian, who shakes their hand and wishes them a warm welcome? If they swear or have no money or they smell or are not polite, will the community invite them back? Alas, we insiders make it abundantly clear that these people are dislocated, out of their element.

I am not suggesting that church people are impolite or unwelcoming. What is said or done to these different or surprising people may be only one way that we keep outsiders at arms length. There are many more subtle ways. Just look at the hymns we sing. How many were written in this century, let alone this decade? How many have tunes that are catchy, well known? (Luther used pub tunes—no wonder he was popular.) How about our prayers? Would a street person recognize themselves in this language? The practice of praying is foreign enough; we cannot expect a stranger to feel "at home" when our vocabulary and symbols are so far removed from the modern context. It is out of frustration over the empty form of much Protestant worship that the recent liturgical renewal is born.

Here is a key question for worship leaders: Does the structure, style, and content of our liturgy, much of which is based on sociological and theological assumptions of the past century, really touch the heart of an outsider? Can we honestly say that our praise of God captures the imagination of a sensitive sceptic or provokes the spiritual surprise that converts the estranged?

Many of us have ceased trying to make our gathering come alive with the fervent energy of a converting company of believers. It is for this reason that cautious searchers may feel uncomfortable walking through our worship space. They have been taught from an early age that their questions, doubts, and yearnings are not welcome here; that by virtue of who they are, they disrupt the regularly greased liturgical machine. There is no place at the table up front for unsettling, unanswerable questions. You could call this an ecclesiastical attitude problem—we are unable to see beyond the superficial to recognize God's surprises underneath. We are unwilling to grant that creation is

GOD HATES RELIGION

more than a static object, one filled with an electric potential for conversion.

A static or fixed view of the created order, a position known in theological circles as "determinism," is the subject of the beginning verses of the Bible. These verses speak of a creation that is "on the way."

The Spirit that Moves

The second verse of Genesis reads, "The Spirit of God moved upon the waters." The author of this first creation story employs the rich Hebrew *ruach,* meaning "breath." It is a very suggestive noun or adjective when applied to the divine. *Ruach* can also be translated as the spirit or essence of the Creator God. This essence is transferred to all living creatures through God's act of creation. Besides these two meanings, *ruach* can be read as wind or breeze. Genesis 1:2 is an example of this rendering of the word. Imagine the echoes of meaning that spread through the first few verses of the Bible when God's breath, spirit, wind, and creative essence "rage over the waters."

While I love the seas, I must confess that my sailing skills are not one of my strong points. I was once out in a storm with my partner, Kelly, sailing a gaff-rigged, six-meter craft—something I had never attempted before—when a raging storm blew up. I managed to drop the boom on her head, steer our boat onto the rocks, lose my grip on the tiller, and allow the jib to flap off into the air. Quite a feat for an amateur.

Of that afternoon's tempestuous events, the brooding clouds and rising winds remain most vivid in my memory. We've all seen a storm, watched the ripples turn to white water, felt the gentle breezes turn into a gale. But watching a gale approach while working the business end of a small sailboat is quite another thing. It is not a pretty sight. A knot tightens in your stomach, sweat breaks out on your brow. Awe and fear, surprise and helplessness, swirl about together.

Hebrew is such a suggestive tongue; it is precisely this sense

SIN AS A STATE OF BEING

of deep awe, mystery, and helpless surprise that the author wants to conjure up. Here we are at the beginning of all things, a profound black beginning that is stirring around, restless and brooding. Over this chaotic, primordial night rushes a great wind, a tempest which is searching, pushing and prying at the edges of the deep chaos. The breath of God, the essence of all living things, looking for a place to begin.

What's the point of this image? What possible message could the author of Genesis want to impart? One interpretation is that everything comes from the eternal. Even before time began, God was and is. There is nothing created that does not originate in the creative power of the Maker of all.

This is a comforting thought. Everyone on earth is a piece of that Creative force and every living being, every rock, tree, and pond can make that claim. It follows that the writer of this creation legend wanted us to appreciate the Creator of all things as a Being that is moving. Creation began through the brooding of God's life force, but it is not finished—ever. Is it possible for us to believe that the tempestuous breath of God is still sweeping across the waters of human civilization, brooding and turbulent? Creation didn't end on the seventh day when God rested. At each sunrise, the world comes alive again. There are surprises peeking out behind every new dawn that even the Almighty may not yet understand.

To believe in the ever-present, creating spirit of God means that we can all take a deep breath and relax. We can stick a label on our faults that reads, "Please be patient, God isn't finished with me yet." The members of the community of believers who trust the Hebrew and Christian Scriptures can never claim to be complete people who have their frayed edges all stitched up. We are a company that admits we have much to learn. Each moment is an opportunity for a new me, for a new world.

In many ways, the electronic age with its urgency, immediacy, and efficiency has affected our ability to experience surprise, to touch the miraculous. Computers are the ultimate tool of predictability. But still we long for spiritual surprises—to be converted and swept away by the passion of a new outlook.

Each December 24, I roam the television channels looking for the Dickens classic, *A Christmas Carol,* starring Alistair Sim. Watching it, I always cry, not because of the poverty, distress, or pain of Tiny Tim, but because of the conversion of Scrooge. Here is the creation story repeating itself. God is far from finished with Ebeneezer. After a night of frightening communion with spirits and confrontations with his own cruelty and hard-heartedness, Ebeneezer pleads: "Spirit!... hear me! I am not the man I was. I will not be the man I must have been but for this intercourse. Why show me this, if I am past all hope?... Assure me that I yet may change these shadows you have shown me, by an altered life."

This could have been a footnote to the Genesis story. God is not finished with the calling forth of both order and surprise from darkness and despair. We are not decided once and for all time. Life is not determined.

Determinism and the Protestant Mind

The Bible contains ideas or principles that do not follow the implications of the Genesis creation story. Determinism is, after all, quite a natural product of the human soul's search for permanence, for a defendable and reassuring structure or purpose to life. Often these devices of an insecure heart were attributed to divine intention. It should not surprise us that God is depicted in Psalms and in the book of Job as an all-controlling Being, one who manipulates even the most minute detail of human existence.

On the basis of this biblical material, fundamentalist and orthodox religious responses have an affinity with a deterministic appraisal of human existence. For instance, the great reformer John Calvin produced what is perhaps one of the chief Protestant examples of a deterministic religious posture, the doctrine of double predestination. Calvin argues that while God's grace is offered to all people, some are unwilling to heed

SIN AS A STATE OF BEING

God's call. Are they deaf? Does God willingly exclude some people? To preserve God's justice and love, Calvin saw that it was necessary to assume that God was not the problem. Some human beings would not accept divine forgiveness because they were "predisposed"; their lives and all their choices, even the choice of accepting God, were predetermined. Some were destined for heaven, others for hell; hence the use of the term "double."

Calvin's doctrine, one which he himself called "terrible," informed puritanism and subsequently a good deal of North American Protestantism. While it has been softened slightly among evangelical conservatives of this land, it is still quite prominent as a paradigm for understanding God's will for human life. For instance, the principle of predestination or determinism lives on in those religious circles where clear distinctions between lost and saved people are made. While extolling the openness of God's salvation, many fundamentalist groups place narrow conditions on the message of God's forgiveness. One must say the right words, live the right life and extol the five fundamentals. If not, one is never going to experience God's salvation.

In the North American world, conservative Protestant energies are often directed towards drawing boundaries around the righteous and unrighteous, with criteria based on human interpretations of the biblical record. Behind an apparently open face lurks a rigid determinism. In most denominations, there are still some people who are excluded because of who they are. Gays and lesbians are still not openly received as welcome members of most churches. The same is true for blacks in certain southern, white denominations. Only recently were divorcées granted the right to remarry in the Pentecostal church.

Many of the Jesus stories were written to highlight his confrontation with the dynamic of determinism as it was experienced in his day. Acceptability or righteousness was not a free-flowing potential, but a predetermined reality. One's station in life dictated acceptability to God. In his culture, sin was

81

GOD HATES RELIGION

not a matter of intention, but rather a state of being.

Sin as a State of Being

If we read between the lines of Paul's letters to the church in Corinth, it seems clear that one of the chief obstacles to their prosperity was the religiously adapted concept of determinism, the notion that sin was inextricably bound up with one's position in the community. If you were a slave, you were a slave; if you were a sinner, you were a sinner. End of argument. Prostitutes, money collectors, people with gross disfigurements were sinners. It mattered little if they were sensitive, caring people, kind and considerate family members. They were sinners. Their disease was a fixture of their society, and it prescribed their behaviour and their religious standing.

In his correspondence with the Corinthians, Paul faces the rigidity of a religious gathering who insist on circumcision and not eating meat sacrificed to idols as prerequisites for righteousness—illustrative of the determinist argument. Behind Paul's admonitions for tolerance, we can hear the questioners from Corinth asking the apostle if there were not some actions that were by their very nature sinful. Aren't some people sinful no matter what they say or do? Paul opened the door on some industrial strength surprises when he preached the message of a Christian community open to all.

The modern egalitarian mind resists this determinist and exclusive attitude. It smacks of judgementalism, the presumption of divine wisdom and the exclusion of others on much more mundane considerations such as social class, family of origin, or occupation. Jesus felt the same way. In fact, many of his sayings were directed against the equation between one's state of being and sin.

SIN AS A STATE OF BEING

The Great Liberation

A rather long passage from Mark illustrates Jesus' resistance to the artificial distinction of purity and impurity, to sin and righteousness. The central question revolves around defilement and what makes one unacceptable.

The Pharisees gather around him, along with some of the scholars, who had come from Jerusalem. When they notice some of his disciples eating their meal with defiled hands, that is to say, without washing their hands (you see, Pharisees and the Judeans generally wouldn't think of eating without first washing their hands in a particular way, always observing the tradition of the elders, and they won't eat when they get back from the marketplace without washing again, and there are many other traditions they cherish, such as the washing of cups and jugs and kettles), the Pharisees and the scholars start questioning him: "Why don't your disciples live up to the traditions of the elders, instead of eating with defiled hands?"

And he answered them, "How accurately Isaiah depicted you phonies when he wrote:

This people honours me with their lips
but their heart stays far away from me.
Their worship of me is empty,
because they insist on teachings that are human
commandments.

You have set aside God's commandments and hold fast to human tradition!"

Or he would say to them, "How expert you've become at putting aside God's commandment to establish your own tradition. For instance, Moses said, 'Honour your father and your mother' and 'Those who curse their father or mother will surely die.' But you say, 'If people say to their father or mother, "Whatever I might have spent to support you is korban"' (which means

83

GOD HATES RELIGION

"consecrated to God"), you no longer let those persons do any-thing for their father and mother. So you end up invalidating God's word with your tradition, which you then perpetuate. And you do all kinds of other things like that!"

Once again he summoned the crowd and would say to them: "Listen to me, all of you, and try to understand! What goes into you can't defile you; what comes out of you can. If anyone has two good ears, use them!"

When he entered a house away from the crowd, his disciples started questioning him about the riddle. And he says to them: "Are you as dim-witted as the rest? Don't you realize that nothing from outside can defile by going into a person, because it doesn't get to the heart but passes into the stomach, and comes out in the outhouse?" (This is how everything we eat is purified.)

And he went on to say, "It's what comes out of a person that defiles. For from out of the human heart issue wicked intentions, sexual immorality, thefts, murders, adulteries, envies, wicked-ness, deceit, promiscuity, an evil eye, blasphemy, arrogance, lack of good sense. All these evil things come from the inside out and defile the person" (Mark 7:1-23, SV).

Here is revolutionary thinking. It is largely lost to modern hearers who have been steeped in the language of individual-ism and freedom, but Jesus is opening the previously locked doors of the dusty and stifling religious holy halls. He suggests that the defiling agents are not material, not centred on exterior appearances, but on internal motivations and unseen spirits. While Jesus put this message clearly, it was certainly evident in the prophets as well. Micah's famous dictum in chapter 6, verse 8, is a good example. The prophet argued that God does not look to outside performance of religious duty, but to the committed, compassionate heart.

In a larger sense, Jesus is arguing with the religious figures of both his day and ours that nothing is fixed, particularly sinful-ness or impurity. No one is required to sin. No one is bound or pre-determined to fall. These are marvellous words of great liberation, rarely heard in a religious world that regarded rules as signs of devotion and serious piety. The many stories of conversion give ample testimony to the power of this message. Jesus was surrounded by a company of forgiven sinners, people who had been told that their physical condition was not a sign of God's disapproval. They were freed from the weight of guilt and told that their station in life did not constitute, in and of itself, defilement.

How can we comprehend this subverting "good news"? As Jesus travels about the conservative region of Galilee, he leaves chaotic restlessness in his wake among many dispossessed peasants. One with "authority" forgives their sins and erases generations of tradition regarding one's fallen or defiled nature. Lepers dance in freedom, women of the night walk proud, tax collectors breathe the intoxicating air free of guilt. *And people are radically changed.* Wherever Jesus went, the surprises never ceased.

As we see the Jesus movement in this light, it is obvious that it had far-reaching political and economic implications. A people no longer bound by spiritually imposed captivity were a dangerously volatile and subversive agent of change.

How do we transcreate the idea of liberation from ontological determination of sin? At first glance, it seems foreign to our context. The closest our context comes to religiously inspired determinism is the treatment of women in our society. Until recently, they were not considered legal entities (Quebec, the last province in Canada to do so, did not declare women to be separate legal entities until 1964!). There are still several states in America where a wife is not allowed to charge her husband with rape. Presumably, since a wife is bound to the husband's will, forced sex is never rape. She has no identity separate from that of the husband.

This attitude is the direct result of centuries of conditioning by the Christian church. Women were to emulate Mary, the mother of Jesus: "Be meek and mild; submit to your husband's authority." That was the dreadful message. Women in our world

GOD HATES RELIGION

know the oppression of determinism. They have been faulted and diminished as a result of who they are, for being women. No matter what women think or believe, no matter what they say or how efficient and clever they may be, they cannot be ordained as priests in the Roman Catholic church, for instance. Only in the last few decades have women begun to break some of the gender barriers in the Protestant church. Yet there are still many examples of believers and communities refusing the services of a female minister.

Women of this era are beginning to experience liberation from the presumption of sin. Many groups still await this liberation—the poor, the homeless, those who face physical or mental challenges, gays and lesbians. Unfortunately, as many realize, they are not welcomed by the followers of Jesus because they do not fit the pre-determined pattern. They are outsiders.

It is certainly more than time for a transformation, for a return to the open ministry of Jesus where one expected to be surprised and was not fooled by exteriors or human standards of acceptability.

"I be two!": The Child-like Church

If we feel like giving up on life's surprises, if we feel that there is no possibility of new life in our denominations, then perhaps emergency measures are necessary. Why don't we stop all our debates, stop pouring energy into buildings and status, and see our world with the eyes of a young child? See how everything is new—the colour of toothpaste, flowers in the vase on the window ledge, a dog's furry coat. It's all fresh, alive, and surprising. Joy and light shine in the strangest places.

Think of the autumn. In that season of the year when things begin to wither and decay, surprises still await us. Can you recall the rich, musty odour of dry leaves? Let it conjure up the haunting mystery of Halloween, a shadowy darkness when nothing is as it seems. Why, there's a whole treat bag full of surprises on that night. How about fall church suppers? Crowds

SIN AS A STATE OF BEING

of adults and children jostling to find a place, church tables bending under the strain of steaming dishes all designed to make your mouth water. And how many pieces of pie did you have—six, seven? My brother once ate seven, grinning from ear to ear. Surprised? I was awe-struck at such an accomplishment. Who can forget the hint of snow in the air, catching us unawares, as if fall would last for ever?

Surprises filled and overflowed the vessel of our childhood. How sad it is that, as we get older, we grow calluses over that part of our soul and no longer feel the resurrection rub of surprise, at least not without a considerable amount of work. But all is not lost. Like many things in life, our surprise ability can be re-learned. Open your eyes. Wonder is waiting for us in the touch of a tiny hand, in the swaying of a birch tree in the autumn twilight, in the liberating laughter of small children. Can't our church try exercising its surprise muscles? Then we could join with Maude, dancing about the kitchen, daring to be foolish, and shouting, "I be two!"

Chapter 6

Respectability and Other Hidden Boundaries

Jesus acted as an alternate boundary keeper in a way subversive to the established procedures of his society.

—Crossan 1994, 82

It is the victims who reveal to us aspects of our own society that are hidden by mainstream culture.

—Baum 1987, 67

Who's Not in the Pews?

We've been examining the once holy church in a largely theoretical fashion. Now I want you to be subjective and imagine going to church on a Sunday morning. How would you feel if you were a street person? Picture yourself wearing a tattered and stained shirt, a coat with a broken zipper, chunky winter boots that drip slush on the red carpet, gloves that have holes worn in the fingers. Suppose you have no job. Suppose you can't afford breakfast. How do you feel as the ushers arrive at your side?

Where does all this discomfort originate? Is it subjective, the projection of your own insecurity before God? Do you create your own dis-ease or do these holy places exude unsettling subliminal messages, whispered echoes from unseen spirits: "You don't belong here"?

RESPECTABILITY AND OTHER HIDDEN BOUNDARIES

Given your dishevelled appearance, how can you feel at home? Who is ready to lay down their weary soul and rest for a moment when the atmosphere is thick with unwritten and immutable "don'ts" and "shouldn'ts"? It isn't easy. It's unconscious and almost automatic. You know you are out of place and sense that everyone is looking at you. Your clothes and your strangeness telegraph your outsider status. Do you have any change for an offering? Will people notice that you haven't been to church for a while, if ever? Are you welcome in the house of God?

If there is one universal criticism levelled at institutional religion within the North American context, it is that there are too many artificial boundaries. Imposed by respectability or piety, these religious walls separate the bright, shining, religious sheep from the unwanted, tarnished goats. It's amazing that, without much training or instruction, outsiders perceive there is a certain comportment, expected behaviour and required dress. Invisible barriers are as common and imposing as locked doors.

The Invisible Boundaries

We who are the insiders see nothing to impede anyone's full participation in the life of the community. We are genuinely astounded when outsiders say they don't feel welcome, since welcome is precisely what we want visitors to feel. Lifetime attenders are unable to recognize that the strongest and most resistant walls in this church are transparent. There are no bouncers at the door on Sunday morning; no list of rules restricting access. Nevertheless, our weekly gatherings have no trouble at all communicating that some people are welcome while others are not. It's all unspoken, and yet it's so clear.

How many church meetings echo with the unsolved mystery of low Sunday attendance? Most commonly, the church building, whether urban or rural, is located in the midst of a sizeable secular population, very few of whom attend the weekly wor-

89

GOD HATES RELIGION

ship service. "Why don't they come?" That's the usual litany. And tortured consciences ask, "What's wrong? What will make people feel welcome here?"

There is a rather obvious answer to the question of non-attendance. Ask yourself if you would walk into a stranger's house uninvited; just waltz in and sit down as if it were your own home. It takes tremendous courage and a highly motivated person to cross the foreboding frontier of privacy. It's not "their place." How or why would they choose to make it their own?

Besides the obvious boundaries of insider/outsider, there are layers of divisions that keep people away from church. Take gainful employment as a case in point, and reflect on the position of an unemployed person. Unlike the Mediterranean world in which Jesus lived, our world assigns honour and shame according to one's capacity to produce. Whereas the people of Palestine linked one's relative importance to family connections, our culture reserves its highest honours for the "doers," the "achievers." We are a "can do" society, and those who can't do, who can't produce anything worth some form of remuneration, are disowned. It's such an obvious standard that we hardly give it a second thought. Long-term unemployed persons are considered to be lazy, unwilling to try hard enough to create their own labour—social leeches. It is not a coincidence that people living on welfare are also the first to be scapegoated when economic trends decline.

Of course, the church never bars its doors to welfare recipients or unemployed workers. On the contrary, we make plenty of sympathetic noises about caring for them, but they are always "them." Listen to our weekly announcements. When matters turn to issues of charity, preachers often assume that food aid or benevolent money are for those outside the church community. Consequently, we never explain such aid in a way that would make it clear to the worshipping community that they could use it should they ever be in trouble. The unspoken message is clear. Unemployed people aren't expected to be part of the church family.

RESPECTABILITY AND OTHER HIDDEN BOUNDARIES

Like many human institutions, churches align themselves according to class interests. The traditional Protestant churches within the North American context have always been upwardly mobile. As an ethic of hard work and frugal living was instilled in adherents, many members of religious reform movements quite naturally grew into economic security. People's lifestyles and income levels rose as the discipline of faith worked its wonders. In many Protestant denominations, such as Methodism and Presbyterianism, this sociological phenomenon was confused with a theological imperative. Religious, virtuous people assumed that their new found wealth was an indication of God's blessing. The comfortable middle- to upper-class status was a reward for moral living. It was an unfortunate equation. As a result, the poor were regarded as unworthy, less than moral. In spite of the wide range of economic levels represented in any church today, and regardless of the fact that many preachers argue that "it's no sin to be poor," there is a subtle yet lasting theologically based prejudice against poverty. It is equated with either God's disfavour or one's unwillingness to work hard enough to earn divine blessings.

Most believers love their house of prayer and yet, looking around, we will see the signs of a well-heeled community— polished wood, perhaps a stained glass window, some brass ornaments. This is not the home of the dispossessed. The architecture says unequivocally, "We have means." Equally evident is an unvoiced message, "Those without means are in the wrong place."

Besides the physical structure, there are signals in the worship services that exclude the poor and unemployed. Churchgoers commonly dress well (read expensively) and this deters those who can't afford to keep up with the high cost of fashion. The offering plate also exercises quite a formidable influence on the gathered community each Sunday morning. Going hand to hand, it declares that the people sitting in the pews have money, enough and to spare. In the ignorance of our affluence, we claim that you don't need to bring an offering, but when the brass

91

GOD HATES RELIGION

plate is coming down the line of believers, it delivers the opposite message: "You'd better have something to put into it." And if the poor have nothing to bring, is it any wonder they stay away in droves?

In a mercantile culture like ours, economic boundaries are the most distinctive and overtly oppressive. Money confers respectability, while poverty engenders ignobility. But there are other boundaries, ones of a strictly religious nature, that also exercise influence in the church family. Those who have broken the moral code, young single mothers for instance, can feel the invisible walls that dissect a church sanctuary. They are on the business end of an unfortunate assumption that if you are not within the social norms, you must have done something "wrong." Such people are not actively solicited as our prospective members. Rather, we keep a wary eye on them or give them a wide berth. Their lives are tainted. Would they be good believers?

In a similar vein, the Protestant church looks with some scorn on smokers and drinkers. Vestiges of past intolerance still linger in the holy spaces of our souls, and while "bad" habits are not a direct affront to the deity or to the religious exercise, such vices demonstrate a willingness to be drawn towards the "pleasures of the flesh."

Touching on the physical raises one of the most pervasive yet unconscious boundaries. Its focus is on purity and impurity. Sexuality and physical acts are the determining factors in establishing the frontiers of acceptable and unacceptable behaviour. Active and openly homosexual persons are still not welcomed in many Christian denominations, except for the Metropolitan Community Church (one expressly having a ministry for and among gays and lesbians). To be gay, for example, and to live in a publicly acknowledged relationship is an anathema for the Christian church. There is no issue which establishes fixed and immovable lines of battle in the company of Jesus as quickly as that of homosexuality. Like a lightning rod, it attracts all of our latent paranoia over bodily functions, corporal existence, and

92

RESPECTABILITY AND OTHER HIDDEN BOUNDARIES

sexual desire—all the things our Christian tradition still regards as unsettling.

While the old mainstream Protestant churches have higher boundaries around economic issues, it is the fundamentalist churches that draw the firmest line between themselves and the homosexual community. Consequently, AIDS and other sexually transmitted diseases are considered defiling agents, not usually desirable in the Christian community. Prostitutes, bar dancers, and other people working the sex trade are equally shunned as undesirable and impure. (We haven't progressed much past the prejudices of the ancient Hebraic world, which excluded women who touched bodily fluids of any kind.) At best, only sex trade workers who are forgiven and converted are accepted.

In a similar vein, though much less rigidly, heterosexual people who live together outside of marriage are suspect. If they are willing to work and show signs of wanting to be married, they may break through to the inner circle. While common-law relationships are normative in the secular world, they are still frowned upon by our church and viewed with suspicion.

A final boundary, one which exists as firmly today as it did in the days of Jesus of Nazareth, is propriety or deference to the holy. Those who wish to be admitted to the inner sanctum must show themselves worthy. Having a polite and appropriately penitent deportment was and is essential. Faith is equivalent to propriety, to respect for the way things are, to not pushing too hard at the edges. The reign of heaven is not open to the vulgar or to those who use foul language or lack the necessary etiquette.

The Curse of Success

The irony is that, as far as can determined, the original community of Jesus comprised the people that his society, and to a lesser extent our own, would reject. The company of the carpenter were outsiders: illiterate fishers, impure tax collectors, de-

93

testable lepers, and undesirable prostitutes. Jesus regularly ate with the people who were shunned by the "righteous" folk of his world.

As mentioned in previous chapters, this openness to the marginalized members of his society was integral to Jesus' ministry. It was symbolized by the open table, the egalitarian feast fellowship (Crossan) that embodied a new reign of God in which all economic or spiritual barriers would be erased. There is little doubt that the very lack of boundaries captured the imagination of Christ's first followers. It was the unique and attractive feature of his mission, one which radiated out into the wider Roman society, bringing liberation to all the lost minorities: the slaves, the uneducated, the women. The dismantling of religious walls is, indeed, a revolutionary act, and it should not surprise us that Jesus was crucified for promoting it.

Initially, rich and poor, priestly and impious, sinner and saved all sat down at a common meal. As the Jesus movement grew, however, it took on the colouring of the patriarchal organizations that were at hand—empires, teacher-disciple schools of philosophy, mystery religions with closely guarded entrance examinations. Regretfully, it seemed natural and desirable that Christ's church should appropriate the familiar and time-tested designs used in other cultural institutions, and boundaries began to creep into the Jesus movement.

Success has been the constant and ironically misunderstood curse of most religious movements within the Judeo-Christian tradition. As with the original movement at the turn of the first century, so it has been with the reformations of the Christian religion. They all began with a strong commitment to an egalitarian, communal model of openness to society's rejected people. Yet each reform movement lost its prophetic edge as it gained success and popularity, succumbing to the more common model of church where lines of inclusion and exclusion were clearly drawn.

In the Methodist tradition that began at the very low levels of society in England, certain types of behaviour soon spelled exclusion from the "respected circle." If you drank excessively, were unemployed and not a hard worker, you were out. The same course of events took place in the Pentecostal movement on this continent.

Walls are usually a response to fear. Religious walls assuage the frightened soul that imagines its salvation depends upon "proper" behaviour. In pre-modern times, believers reflected on the cycle of seasons, the bounty of creation, and assumed that its benevolence was hanging by the thread of right ritual. The gods would bless the earth only if the sacrificial rite went according to plan. In the Judeo-Christian tradition, walls were built to protect order and purpose. The continuation of the covenant was dependent on our actions and a scrupulous adherence to prescribed lifestyles. Consequently, our spiritual and physical purity were central religious imperatives. We kept impure people out and retained an inner purity to preserve God's favour. Whatever the tradition, the boundaries are delineated to keep the community intact and free of blemish. This religious thinking links divine favour and human action. In the secular myths of the modern culture, we hear a similar message: "He knows when you've been sleeping, he knows when you're awake. He knows when you've been bad or good, so be good for goodness sake."

In the gospel records, there are numerous accounts of Jesus crossing over the line that separated sinner from saved. He consistently broke down the barriers of fear and undermined the self-centred religious thinking that made God's love dependent on human behaviour.

Given the minority images employed by Jesus, I wonder if he expected his followers to succeed. Was he hoping for respectability or for an institution safe enough to be given tax concessions and social privileges? Perhaps those who declare themselves to be outside the bounds of the "acceptable" and, therefore, not welcome in church are more reflective of the original intention of the Saviour than those who bask in relative comfort on "the inside."

GOD HATES RELIGION

Prophetic Imagination

It is difficult to unearth the original intentions of Jesus, to know what he wanted to see happen through his ministry or if he had a change of heart along the way. It does appear by his actions that he attacked or undermined the myriad of boundaries of piety and privilege that transected his society. That he challenged the religious establishment from a base among the peasants and the rejects is not at all surprising; after all, he was a peasant himself. In company with the other great prophets, he did not preach easy salvation to the affluent and spiritual elite, but good news to the poor and impure.

There are two dimensions of the prophetic Hebraic heritage with which Jesus is in continuity. In the first place, prophecy was not so much a matter of substance as it was of perspective. Prophecy was a divergent, subversive imagination, a way of seeing and imagining the world (see Bruggemann). Micah, Amos, Jeremiah, Isaiah, Hosea all saw the world from God's perspective, as it was meant to be. They spoke of a realm of shalom, where everyone had enough, no one had too much, and fear was banished. It was this vision of a new divine reign on earth that characterized the unique message that Christ proclaimed.

In opposition to the dominant "monarchical" or "imperial" vision, the prophets saw with the eyes of a God who cried out for justice. To exercise this prophetic imagination was to see the evil of a social structure patterned after the pretence of pious power and political privilege. It was to declare the coming of the day of the Lord—that moment when such false boundaries would be torn apart.

In continuity with the prophets, Jesus also considered the poor and powerless to be the yardstick of a prophetic imagination. It was a society's treatment of its disenfranchised that determined a community's relative righteousness or impurity. The God of the biblical tradition was not happy with rivers of ceremonial oil or endless sacrifices but longed only for justice

RESPECTABILITY AND OTHER HIDDEN BOUNDAR.

and mercy. How were the least of the community treated? Did they have their just share within the community's life? Was the common table open for them? These were the primary questions, the touchstones of truth. Consequently, the prophets spoke from among the powerless, not because the powerless were more virtuous, but because it was their treatment or mistreatment, their inclusion or exclusion, that was at issue.

In a similar fashion, liberation theologians argue that God has taken a preferential option for the poor; taking their side, their experience, as primary. God's reign, if it is to come at all, must have its heartbeat among these people.

By including everyone at his table, no matter what their station or virtue, Jesus was functioning in the prescribed manner of the prophet who defied false boundaries. The meal fellowship was key to his ministry, a re-enactment of the original shalom concept—no distinctions, no boundaries. Of course, it was often the marginalized and lost folk who stayed at the table to listen to the conversation. The rough peasant and hopeless blind beggar, decidedly unrighteous people, were the first to seek liberation from the false barriers of religion.

This orientation towards a community without boundaries has always posed difficulties, not for the outsiders particularly, for they reject religion even as they have been rejected. No, the gospel message of tearing down the religious walls was and is troubling for the insiders. If God is visible among the marginalized, with the one sheep who is lost, so to speak, what does that say about the ninety and nine who stayed in the fold? Have you ever been troubled by your insider status? Where is the place of the loyal church member in the coming reign of God? We love this institution. Is it possible that the boundary-less community of faith is a challenge to a new way of being church? Do we need to be born again? I believe that this is, indeed, the hope of the gospel for the powerful and righteous: "You must be born again."

n the religious community has reshaped the origi-
subtly refining the stories so that the threat of a
out boundaries is diminished or dismissed. The
nativity story is a good example of how the subversive content
of our heritage has been domesticated and the danger of openness controlled.

God Chooses Insignificance: Luke's Riddle

Here's a riddle: the secret of living is recognizing what you
think, not thinking what you recognize. You may have to re-run
that a few times before it sinks in. How often do we approach
life assuming we will learn what we already know?

Take Christmas, for instance. As the season draws near, the
lights go on and the nativity scenes come out. Who can miss
them? Even those among us who are not Christian see what they
expect to see: the stylized statues of the holy family. There's
Joseph, a ruggedly calm and reassuringly strong father, extending a helping hand. At his feet, the baby Jesus—a cuddly, perfect
child, as happy in cold straw as most are in warm flannel
pyjamas. "No crying he makes." And who would mistake Mary,
the perfect mother, clothed in serenity and grace?

As we pass a crèche by the church or in our homes, we glance
down and see what we know. Joseph is kind, a solid, dependa-
ble type. Jesus is a blessing come to earth, a pure gift. And Mary
is meek and submissive. Isn't that the picture?

But is that really the scene? Is that what the gospel actually
tells us about this family? What does Mary say that leads us to
recognize her as the mild-mannered mother and model of humility for all young women? Apart from a few references in
which she complains of Jesus being too distant from his family
of origin, Mary only speaks once in the Gospels. Actually, it's a
song found in Luke's account of Christ's birth. Without doubt,
the best, most comprehensive record of her thoughts is found in
a stunning poem called "The Magnificat."

At that time Mary set out in haste for a town in the hill country of Judah, where she entered Zechariah's house and greeted Elizabeth. And it so happened, when Elizabeth heard Mary's greeting, the baby jumped in her womb. Elizabeth was filled with holy spirit and proclaimed at the top of her voice, "Blessed are you among women, and blessed is the fruit of your womb! Who am I that the mother of my lord should visit me? You see, when the sound of your greeting reached my ears, the baby jumped for joy in my womb. Congratulations to her who trusted that what the Lord promised her would come true."

And Mary said, "My soul extols the Lord, and my spirit rejoices in God my Savior, for he has shown consideration for the lowly status of his slave. As a consequence, from now on every generation will congratulate me; The Mighty One has done great things for me, and holy is his name, and his mercy will come to generation after generation of those who fear him. He has shown the strength of his arm, he has put the arrogant to rout, along with their private schemes; he has pulled the mighty down from their thrones, and exalted the lowly; he has filled the hungry with good things, and sent the rich away empty. He has come to the aid of his servant Israel, remembering his mercy, as he spoke to our ancestors, to Abraham and to his descendants forever." And Mary stayed with her about three months, and then returned home (Luke 1:39-56, SV).

What is she saying? There are certainly some phrases at the beginning which portray her as a duly thankful servant of God. "Who me? You want to choose me to change the world?" She's surprised and a bit overwhelmed. While Mary submits to God's power and purpose, she hardly appears to be the serene maidservant. She is humble, but never humiliated.

What do we make of the lines about scattering "the proud in the imagination of their hearts," and pulling down "the mighty from their thrones?" King Herod wouldn't hear that as "meek and mild." It's treasonous and downright rebellious. A political manifesto to equal the communist one. In Mary's vision of

GOD HATES RELIGION

God's rule, powerful and proud people will lose status and their exclusivity and privileges will be taken away. Inequalities will be levelled off; the lowly will rise as the rich fall.

What do we make of her notion that Gods fills "the hungry with good things" and sends the rich away empty? Now that's uncomfortable for many of us. I am relatively rich by the world's standards, with an education, a job, a house. Will God really send away wealthy individuals like myself and give special attention to poor people?

In the past, church leaders have, perhaps inadvertently, softened the edges of Mary's Song by suggesting that it is a spiritual psalm of praise copying one voiced by Hannah (1 Sam. 1:11; 2:1-10) or another sung by Judith (Judith 13:18; 16:11). Both were sung as laments of a lost and confounded people. Luke does portray Mary as a spiritual being, and her words hold powerful meaning for the human heart. Yet I believe Luke intended to portray Mary's Song as more than a psalm of praise to God. This isn't just a religious song. While Mary was not only referring to economic realities when she thanked God, it cannot be ignored that, in her day, such neat distinctions between religion and politics were non-existent. To speak spiritually was to refer also to earthly affairs and vice versa. The two were intertwined.

That's the riddle. What is the point of this poem—spiritual obedience or political renewal? Mary came from a poor part of the world. Galilee was regularly oppressed by absentee landlords and marauding armies of occupation. Whether Mary actually spoke these words, a fact doubted by most biblical scholars, they were obviously central to Luke's vision for him to place them in the mouth of the mother of our Lord. So it is unimportant whether it was Mary herself or Luke who coined the phrases. The words have a power all their own. Mary meant what she said. Her child was to be an invitation to liberation, spiritual, yes, but also quite concrete and real. Jesus was real bread for the hungry and lively hope for the poor. He would re-order the social and theological landscape, undermining the pretentious boundaries that separated rich and poor, noble and humble.

RESPECTABILITY AND OTHER HIDDEN BOUNDARIES

Mary's Song issues a warning to monarchs, prime ministers, presidents, priests, and to all those who wish to lord it over the weak. Your time is coming—all the clear boundaries will be thrown out.

And it didn't end with Mary. Her song is etched throughout Luke's Gospel. This bias is evident from the beginning when, in contrast to Matthew, Luke begins his nativity story with the birth of Jesus in a manger. Homeless and vulnerable, Mary and Joseph are not visited by exotic nobles from another world or sought after by mighty kings. That's the vision of the First Gospel. Luke's holy parents travel as unknowns, attended by shepherds, the ancient equivalent of parking lot attendants. They were nobodies. There are no great tumultuous events, no regal authorities rushing to forestall the baby's arrival. He was born in a cow stall in a backwater little town.

Beyond the birth narratives, Luke portrays Jesus as a man in continuity with the prophet Isaiah. The carpenter from Galilee starts his ministry with the declaration that "the spirit of the Lord is upon me, because he has anointed me to bring good news to the poor. He has sent me to announce pardon for prisoners and recovery of sight to the blind; to set free the oppressed, to proclaim the year of the Lord's amnesty" (Luke 4:18-19, SV). This speech in Nazareth sets the tone and acts as a mission statement, so to speak, for the ministry of Jesus (one that still seems adequate today, by the way). Luke recounts this interest in the rejected outsiders throughout his gospel, including certain passages and stories unique to his writing—the good Samaritan, the prodigal son, Zaccheus, and the plight of Lazarus.

Church: A Community Where There Is No Distinction

The general message of the reign of God as far as Luke is concerned is clear, and the Magnificat sets the tone. In God, there are no distinctions. Any pretence of importance or righteousness or respectability is irrelevant to the Creator of all.

It is not surprising that the oppressed of Latin America have

GOD HATES RELIGION

worshipped and devoted their lives to Mary. She speaks to them of their pain, of the imposition of unfair barriers and of the eventual liberation from destructive walls. Mary and all the outsiders who have been victimized by the religious barriers reveal to the insiders, to the wall builders, who we are. The well-being of the outsider is the measuring stick of our health. Keeping "them" out will be our spiritual and physical death. Surely the health of the company of Jesus rests on the constant and intentional inclusion of the people the world rejects. Our future well-being will continue to depend on breaking down the walls that divide us.

When you pass by a crèche, whether you are Christian or not, look at Mary and know what you see. Here is a rebel who breaks down the barriers of respectability and status. Here is a woman who, though marginalized by her own community, is bold and courageous enough to declare that God will level hurtful distinctions and empower the lowly. Indeed she is blessed.

Chapter 7

Just Us versus Justice

Students of a wise rabbi once asked, "Master, when do we know the dawn is coming and night is past? Is it when we can tell a sheep from a goat even though they are out in the pasture? Is it when we can distinguish an oak from a cedar tree?" "No," the Rabbi replied. "You know a new day is breaking when you can look into the eyes of a stranger and see your brother or your sister. Until that time comes, we are still in the night."

—Ancient rabbinic story

The Church as Social Club

Imagine that you are a visitor seated in a hushed and hallowed sanctuary. Easter Sunday service is about to begin. What do you feel? You have an interest in spiritual matters, but you've never joined a church family.

Do you feel out of place, impure, perhaps less virtuous or pious than you should be? Do you feel welcome? There was a smile at the door, a warm handshake, but they can wear off by the time you find a seat. Is this your place? Maybe you are shifting about in your seat, sensing that somehow you are out of your depth.

This would not be surprising, would it? For there is a barrier that goes beyond questions of morality, economics, or social class, one which is often invisible to the church-goer. It is a spiritual distinction: the "at home" qualification. North Ameri-

GOD HATES RELIGION

can churches are based on this division, with a great divide separating members and strangers.

In theological terms, it is known as the distinction between the visible and the invisible church. During the Christendom era, when mainstream Protestantism was given everything short of official status, everyone was nominally "Christian." The "visible" church, the actual people who visited the church building and attended the sacraments, was not equivalent to the "invisible" church, the body of believers who accepted the true belief, who were the saved and righteous in God's sight. On any given Sunday, the worshipping congregation was a mixture of both.

Splinter groups often tried to close the gap and build communities of faith that comprised both the visible and invisible church. However, you couldn't be a member of these sects unless you were declared fit. You had to prove yourself worthy according to a pre-determined standard of righteousness. In these churches, strangers were welcome only if they converted and conformed to a code of behaviour. Searching and earnest souls were admitted, but with probationary standing. This discouraged foreigners and other unwanted types from intruding on the purity of the gathering community.

What began as a distinctive posture of the right end of the religious spectrum has become an unacknowledged reality for all Christian organizations. As North American society grows into a more secular and pluralistic maturity, the Christian church is no longer the agent of social adhesion. It is more often than not an ethnic enclave, reflecting class and economic homogeneity. Contrary even to the wishes of the denominations involved, the pews have become more and more reserved for acceptable and recognized people. Foreigners are not expected to attend. This closed ecclesiastical posture can be so exaggerated that a community of faith devolves into a pious social club, a world within a world where you know you're known and accepted.

But what happens to outsiders and foreigners in this circumstance? In the one place where one would hope to find a welcome for the strangers at the gate, there is suspicion and mistrust.

JUST US VERSUS JUSTICE

All too often our community of faith is more concerned with preserving its own internal cohesiveness than professing a community open to all.

There is considerable criticism of closed religion in the Bible. To the extent in which faith serves an elite community, it runs contrary to God's original intention regarding strangers and people with no rights (see Ex. 22:21-24; Deut. 24:17-19). This criticism is precisely the point of Mark's parable of the cure of the Greek woman's daughter.

> From there he got up and went away to the regions of Tyre. Whenever he visited a house he wanted no one to know, but he could not escape notice. Instead, suddenly a woman whose daughter had an unclean spirit heard about him, and came and fell down at his feet. The woman was a Greek, by race a Phoenician from Syria. And she started asking him to drive the demon out of her daughter. He responded to her like this: "Let the children be fed first, since it isn't good to take bread out of the children's mouths and throw it to the dogs!"
>
> But as a rejoinder she says to him, "Sir, even the dogs under the table get to eat scraps ⟨dropped by⟩ children."
>
> Then he said to her, "For that retort, be on your way, the demon has come out of your daughter."
>
> She returned home and found the child lying on the bed and the demon gone (Mark 7:24-30, SV).

One of the criteria for determining the historical authenticity of Jesus' pronouncements is that of "embarrassment." It is argued that a gospel writer would not make up something that portrays Jesus in a poor light. Therefore, if a text is unflattering, it may have some historical authority; otherwise why repeat it? On the basis of the criteria of embarrassment, this text from Mark may well contain a kernel of historical truth. It is certainly not flattering. Rather than being the open and universal saviour, Jesus is depicted as having a rather narrow parochial concern for the people of Israel. His vision does not go beyond the circle

105

GOD HATES RELIGION

of his own clan; strangers are not in line for God's justice.

Was Jesus initially restrictive? Was it Paul and others like him that took the message of the coming reign of God to the lands outside Palestine? Certainly the Acts of the Apostles gives testimony to a certain conflict over the mission to outsiders, gentiles and strangers. In that text Peter and other leaders in Jerusalem had a good deal of difficulty when foreigners claimed membership in the company of Jesus.

It is difficult to sort through the distortions laid upon the gospel narrative by the burgeoning Christian church and uncover its original style. It may well be that the universalism of the Christian church, the assumption that Christ came to save all people, was a relatively late addition. At the time the church became the official religion of the Roman empire, this open gospel was so self-evident that it was written back into the first-century story. Now it is such a common assumption that most believers would have difficulty sorting out fact from fiction.

Clearly, Jesus' mission was primarily to the Jews of Galilee and, to a much lesser extent, to those of Judea. There is no evidence that he preached to foreign crowds. Moreover, his parables, sermons, and sayings seem to be directed at an audience steeped in the Hebraic tradition. No matter how much we might want him to be a modern evangelist saving the souls of the unwashed masses, the rabbi from Galilee appears to have been selective in his mission. He strove to live out a message of a new reign of God, which was coming to reform the Jewish community. Like a great banquet feast, this coming rule of heaven would level artificial boundaries among the chosen people and restore every one to an equal footing before God. That's the main course. According to Mark 7:27, strangers were only entitled to what few crumbs might fall from this table of fellowship. The world's salvation was subservient, if not irrelevant, to the salvation of the nation of Israel.

Feminist scholars have pointed out that this Phoenician woman from Syria challenged that restrictive vision. She is the only person within Mark to encounter the rabbi from Nazareth, clear-

106

JUST US VERSUS JUSTICE

ly disagree with him, and win the argument. It would not be a exaggeration to claim that Jesus is converted through their exchange, albeit in a seemingly grudging manner. Indeed, she may have altered Jesus' understanding of his own ministry. It took a foreign woman asking for inclusion in God's healing designs for the restrictive and confined thinking of a itinerant Jewish preacher to be opened to the just demands of a foreign world.

Can you sense the turmoil this anecdote must have caused among "the twelve" who began to control the Jesus movement in Jerusalem shortly after the crucifixion-resurrection event? Think of them spending hours in debate over whether it was possible that this reign of God proclaimed by Jesus was to touch the stranger as well as the Jew. What seems to us a logical step was, for the first apostles of Christ, a radical departure, for it implied a fundamental shift in thinking. In their minds, the message of the coming "kingdom of heaven" was an issue for insiders, an internal reform of the ancient tradition of Israel. Once this egalitarian vision is imputed to foreigners, the basic assumptions change. At that point we are no longer speaking of a reform of Judaism, a sect-like derivation. If the gospel is for strangers, then the movement that preaches it begins to look like a new religion, a potentially distinct and competing alternative to the old way. It's no wonder Peter and the twelve resisted this expansion.

It was Paul who had the courage to take the message of Jesus to its logical conclusion. If the spiritual barriers within the tradition were to be breached, then surely this would also hold true for the protective religious walls that encircled the Hebraic faith. They also needed to be broken down so that strangers and foreigners could benefit from the message of liberation. When I consider what a similar shift in the religious thinking of our present context might mean, I am astounded at Paul's zealous courage and audacious insight.

Most sermons on the early missionary activities conclude at this point. Paul took the gospel message to foreigners—end of

107

GOD HATES RELIGION

story, end of innovation. But there was a rather significant alteration in the message, one almost entirely ignored by believers and scholars alike, between Jesus and his followers. In Matthew, Mark, and Luke, the preacher from Galilee speaks almost exclusively about a coming reign of God and the community it would engender. His miracles, healings, and actions all reflect that central message. Jesus' messiahship is derivative of that primary vision and he almost never alludes to himself as the spiritual founder or the fountainhead of a new religion. It was initially Paul, and then Peter and the other apostles, who preached about "Jesus, the anointed One of God, as source of eternal Salvation." When Jesus becomes Christ, the message and tone of the gospel is fundamentally altered. What began as a spiritual renewal based upon a re-appreciation of God's justice and love becomes a new religion founded on the acceptance of dogmatic propositions. The gospel of justice is overpowered by the evangelistic necessity to define, expand, and preserve the concept of "just us."

Paul's innovation was a brilliant practical application of Jesus' original vision, an expansion that took seriously the kernel of his message: that all people could approach God without fear or mediation. Nevertheless, the shift of the gospel's central orientation from spiritual freedom to Christ-centred religious affiliation may be a regrettable distortion. It has meant that, for the majority of the church's life span, excessive energy has been spent in preserving the institution, imposing its doctrines on insiders and outsiders alike. The living out of the new reign of God on earth has been discarded as a guiding light. And because the institution has expended its resources in self-preservation, there has been very little tolerance or time for strangers, for those who do not want to "join" the religion. There has been almost no interest in exploring what faith might be like separate from a church structure.

With an appreciation of this dramatic shift in the gospel paradigm, we have returned to the predicament of the modern age. All too often our hymns, prayers, sermons, and sacraments

108

JUST US VERSUS JUSTICE

assume that Jesus was white, middle class, polite, clean, mildly witty, and respectable and that his ultimate concern was with the building up of an organization that used his name. Most of these categories are erroneous cultural mis-readings of the Jesus story. I have little doubt that he would look very much like a stranger in our midst, unable to comprehend either our spiritual symbols or church structures. As much as we might declare ourselves to be his people, he wouldn't fit in easily.

If the gospel narrative is accurate at all, this Jesus of Nazareth would come to us in the modern church as he did to the religious people of his own day and demand a general suspension of institutional preoccupations. Away with the membership drives, bake sales, and the myriad of other activities designed to perpetuate the church organization! The primary role of a community of faith is to promote belief in God the Creator and to live out that faith in a practical and just manner. A church institution is but one tool among many available for that central task.

The Unchurch Church

As the Protestant church is more and more marginalized in the North American context, its chief challenge is to engage strangers in questions of faith without assuming or desiring their membership in our religious club. Can the church function as an unchurch and set aside concerns for its own self-preservation long enough to explore the ways in which the reign of God that Jesus described may dwell among us?

This will be a terribly difficult piece of work since the "Jesus Saves," build-up-the-membership gospel has been firmly imprinted on our hearts. Asking a church to suspend this preoccupation is tantamount to requiring it to set aside its reason for being. On a deeper level it becomes doubly difficult because this declaration of Christ's Lordship supports a host of triumphal images that have powered the tradition for centuries. Where would we turn for succour, comfort, and hope if Jesus was no

GOD HATES RELIGION

longer extolled as the Way, the Truth, and the Life (John 14:6)? Would we not be forsaking the very heart of the faith, abandoning that which makes us unique as a religion?

There are no easy answers to the questions I have raised. And while I trust their direction, I have no assurance of finding acceptable solutions. We live with such a short appreciation of the historical journey of faith that errors in judgement await us at every twist in the road. Nevertheless, our present predicament of decline may be an invitation to change, a call from God to give up our life as an organization for the sake of the renewal of the world's life.

Who can miss the fact that there are many people in our world who long to speak of spiritual matters, yet who have no immediate interest in joining a religion? The shining promise of the age of progress has become tarnished and many are searching for more substance, for trustworthy meaning. Questions of ethical behaviour, just relationships, and spiritual stability are evident in all walks of life. A glance at a list of best-selling books reveals the search for depth and purpose. More and more agencies are concerned with ethics, and the ecological movement, in its reverence for the earth, is one of the most spiritual innovations of this century. All of these themes are matters with which the church has been preoccupied for centuries, and I sense that we are facing a window of opportunity for dialogue.

We must be cautious and respectful, for many of these spiritual pilgrims are not seeking their salvation within the body of Christ. Whether adherence to a community of faith might be salvific or not, they are reluctant to join us. Do we ignore this secular hunger and continue to restrict our affirmations and discussions to our own institutional circles? Can the message of Jesus speak to the foreigners beyond our walls? Do we have an obligation to be concerned about the health of the world? Could it be that these strangers are challenging us much like the Syro-Phoenician woman did Jesus? Is it possible for the church to become de-institutionalized for the sake of participating in a great debate about faith taking place beyond its walls?

JUST US VERSUS JUSTICE

We must not be too naive. The world is not waiting with bated breath for the church to come out from behind its protective shell. The round of spiritual explorations will continue quite well whether we participate or not. But I imagine we would not be unwelcome and might well, with a measure of humility and self understanding, find a useful place in that circle.

A church that lives for the world and not itself—a novel idea.

Chapter 8

Puritanism, Legalism, and Apocalypticism

Puritanism: the haunting fear that someone, somewhere, may be happy.

—H. L. Mencken

Can We Treat the Bible as Rule Book?

Let us assume for a wild moment that we who are spiritual seekers and doubters have overcome the barriers blocking our inclusion in the church community. We no longer feel like the unrighteous, like threatening outsiders who don't fit.

Let's relax our defensive reflexes and imagine our way into the sacred space that surrounds us. The pews are warm. A dusty, lived-in odour drifts by. You can feel your shoulders drooping into that Friday-evening-before-the-television peacefulness. The stiffness drains from your neck as you crane about to enjoy the light refracted through the stained glass. God is in this place, perhaps not where "He" is deemed to be, but present nonetheless.

Can you feel the stirring of something deep within? Like the murmur of lingering spirits long disembodied or the featherlight rustle of angels' wings, something that soothes your soul? Perhaps it's the supple shades of colour or the hushed hint of ancient rites. Perhaps it's the well-worn pews. In the quiet, this space asserts its influence, testimony to generations of worship. By casting off our shyness, we can drink it in, and let that deep and incomprehensible sigh of contentment come out. Isn't it the delicate play of shadow and luminescence and the silence so full of whispers that calls to us? While it may be for only a brief interlude, "it" is here, what we've been looking for and have never found—that much is certain.

As we linger in the beauty of this transcendent moment, we ask ourselves: "Is there anything that might still keep me from joining this community of Christ's disciples?" How about the religious laws, all the guilt-inducing rules of the religiously devout life? Now that you're relaxed, do your many "indiscretions" hover around, unwanted guests at this feast of the soul? Even while we can't remember how many or what they are, we know that we haven't kept the commandments as well as we should. Religious spaces often do that. They make us feel small, frail, and unfinished.

Let's ponder this. Aren't there a lot of regulations that the Bible lays down, rules about dating, bad language, alcohol, gambling, and smoking? Isn't there a rule around the "L" word, "lust"? Isn't it bad? Rising up from Sunday school lessons now long forgotten is the ghost-like phrase, "Lusting after things of the flesh." The preaching voice of the teacher drones on: "The Bible tells us not to covet our neighbour's wife, husband, team of oxen, golf clubs, hockey skates, or convertible." (It went something like that.) And doesn't the same "good book" also say something about drunkenness? Isn't liquor the drink of the devil? Somewhere in my past, I heard, "Don't ask what you are drinking out of the bottle. Ask yourself what the bottle is drinking out of you."

Furthermore, there must be some commandment forbidding religious people to enjoy erotic art. That's a law unto itself. Sexual stimulation, even visual, is much too dangerous for mortals. Such pleasure is perverse unless it can somehow be attached to devotion to God. Hence, the *Song of Songs*, Solomon's passionate love poetry, was explained as a long allegorical piece of pietism describing the love between disciple and Christ.

Aren't all these rules pre-conditions for being "religious?"

GOD HATES RELIGION

Isn't it true that the commandments were written to ensure the denial of the inner passions and the purification of the body? Don't we all ask ourselves, "Can I sit in the pews and not respect the rules, let alone keep them?" Most organizations have a set of by-laws. If you want to belong, you follow the rules. After all, the National Hockey League has an official rule book, pages and pages of what you can and cannot do, on and even off the ice. Football, soccer, baseball, basketball; almost every sport has it's authoritative regulations or codes. Similarly, social clubs, service organizations, professional societies, all have their policy manuals.

Isn't religion the same? Don't devout believers have a rule book to which we can and should turn when someone is playing unfairly or when someone gets injured in a foul move? Aren't we supposed to refer to our commandments, discover the statutes that make living manageable and orderly? Doesn't the religious life demand law? Christians have commonly turned the Bible into a code of regulations that govern life. On a superficial level, Holy Scripture seems to contain all the commandments, formulas, and statutes that any human could possibly need, a collection of "shoulds" for the game of life.

However, this living-by-the-rules approach to the Christian Scriptures is an inappropriate and potentially misguided use of these holy books. The Bible is a text that captures the great poetry of creation. Its holiness does not reside in its rules, but rather in its testimony to the One who "made heaven and earth" (Psa. 121). These books are first and foremost testimonies to the people's faith in an actively compassionate Creator. All the commandments are clearly derivative and secondary to the central proclamation that God is One and God is loving. The purpose of the Scriptures is to turn your heart and mind towards the Maker of the Universe. Rules are just one tool among many for accomplishing that feat.

Take the topic of homosexuality, for example. Often when Christians debate the appropriateness of same-sex relationships or lifestyles, they quote Scripture, believing that citing a dispar-

PURITANISM, LEGALISM, AND APOCALYPTICISM

aging verse from Leviticus or Romans resolves the issue and provides us with a rule. "Homosexuality is a sin." Christians then feel they have done their duty.

While concentration on a specific phrase or sentence within a piece of Scripture has an appealing, "common sense" quality, it is inadequate to the complexity of the questions that face us in the modern context. With regard to homosexuality, there is a major difficulty facing those who would claim to read the Bible and follow it like a set of regulations for living. These folk must ask themselves why they have chosen to ignore certain parts of Scripture, some very clear and detailed rules, while latching tenaciously onto the ones that condemn, for example, homosexual behaviour.

For instance, there are several rather "interesting" laws about not mixing substances. Leviticus 19:19 (just a few verses away from those dealing with two men sleeping together) forbids the mingling of different seeds in sewing or the mixing of linen with wool in the fabrication of garments. We obviously don't take that rule too seriously. And what happened to the economic commandments of Deuteronomy 15:1, which declare that every creditor shall write off all loans in the seventh year? Mortgages are to be forgiven as well—wouldn't that work wonders for our banking system. Why has this commandment been ignored? Then turn to Paul's first letter to the Church in Corinth. He directs that women should remain silent in church assemblies for "it is a shame for women to speak in the church" (14:34). I don't know any self-respecting Christian community of faith that would try to impose that rule.

Why do we disregard these other regulations, and yet hold fast to the ones on certain "deviant" sexual behaviours? If you're going to use the Bible as a rule book, or outline your faith with hard-edged legalism, you had better give thought to why some rules are placed front and centre while others are side-lined.

There are some believers who respond to the seeming inequality of weight given to particular rules by arguing that Jesus "set aside" certain unnecessary ceremonial laws, while main-

115

GOD HATES RELIGION

taining as authoritative other moral commandments of the Hebrew Scriptures. Apart from the fact that we have no record of Jesus making that precise distinction about the Scriptures' laws (see Matt. 5:18: "I swear to you, before the world disappears, not one iota, not one serif, will disappear from the Law," SV), there is evidence that he was prepared to set aside *either* ceremonial or moral commandments, depending on the circumstance. For example, he suspended the moral code on adultery when he did not condemn the woman "caught in adultery," a story found in John 7:53-8:11. He takes similar action in forgiving the prostitute at Simon's house (see Luke 7:36-50). Clearly Jesus' treatment of the law was asymmetrical, not as mechanistic as the simple distinction between moral and ceremonial law might suggest.

There is a second problem with relying solely on the Bible as a code book to direct us with good solid laws by which to live. Often the Scripture's view of what is essential and important runs contrary to our own. That's not surprising, since it was written both within and for a much different social context. On the question of homosexuality, it is clear that the Bible doesn't consider same-sex attraction important enough to be a subject for much debate. At the outside, there are seven or eight references to male homosexual behaviour and only one vague phrase referring to females who seek the company of other women. In a book of many thousands of rules, hundreds of pages, scores of poems, homosexuality is a very small matter indeed, irrelevant as an issue facing the people of that time. The ancient Hebrew language doesn't even have a word for "homosexual" and never mentions the possibility of lesbianism.

Can we make a claim that a handful of verses constitute the basis on which to make an ethical judgement about gays and lesbians? Some would respond that homosexuality is such an obvious affront to God that we don't need more than a few lines to direct us, but one must be careful when advancing that argument. The Bible says a great deal that implicitly favours the institution of slavery, condoning it often, directing the care and protection of slaves, never condemning it as a clearly oppressive

116

PURITANISM, LEGALISM, AND APOCALYPTICISM

social structure. And yet we consider slavery to be such an obvious contradiction of God's love and justice that we ignore all that the Bible has to say in its defence.

In a similar fashion, many church communities have turned a deaf ear to the Scripture's injunctions concerning women and their exclusion from worship. Paul's admonitions about females needing to wear hats in church (1 Cor. 11:4-12) conformed to the fashion of the earlier part of this century, but are systematically ignored today.

Where does that leave the Bible as a rule book when we have used our human judgement to suspend certain clear biblical imperatives? If many churches have, after due consideration, disregarded the Holy Book's patriarchal injunctions against women, for instance, why are we so reluctant to apply the same thinking to the treatment of homosexuals?

Perhaps we have read the current sexual anxiety, often felt most deeply by men, back into a few feeble, biblical references and then assured ourselves of our own prejudices. This is an injustice to the Scriptures. There may be many people who have difficulty accepting the "naturalness" or "health" of homosexual lifestyles, but those are extra-scriptural philosophical points of view. You can peer into the Scriptures and see what you want, no question. But we must ask ourselves if it will be a faithful use of God's word and a legitimate response to the question at hand.

There once was a great Christian preacher who said the Bible is a bit like a mirror: "If a donkey looks in, can we expect a saint to look out?" Quite obviously all believers have been, and are, selective in their reading of the rules in the Bible and biased in their selection of "binding" laws by cultural and societal standards. Regrettable as this may seem, it is unlikely to change as long as human beings are human beings. We are contextual creatures, gaining our perspectives and our sense of significance from our conditioning and culture. It is naive, indeed, to hope for a completely value-free reading of Holy Scripture. That is beyond our finite condition.

GOD HATES RELIGION

Wisdom rests in being aware of those tendencies or prejudices we bring to the reading of God's word. Hopefully we will be able to curb our worst distortions and have enough humility never to claim absolute understanding.

Legalism: The Tyranny of Rules and Regulations

While it is sometimes scandalous and often dangerous to treat the Bible as a rule book, not all the regulations and commandments in the Holy Scriptures can be disregarded. We might well ask ourselves how spiritual and ecclesiastical energy ought to be expended on the rules of religion. Are laws to be followed strictly, suspended when convenient, or interpreted contextually? Do we try to be like Jesus and follow exactly what he said on any given subject? Surely the Bible must offer some direction for believers when it comes to the commandments and what is expected of us.

There are two poles of interpretation regarding the law: at the left end is situationalism and at the right, legalism. The legalist reads the commandments in an "accepted," usually literalist, manner, seeking to follow all the details of the laws (or a specific number of them) with unbending obedience. The holiness code in Leviticus (Lev. 11-27) is one example of a legalistic approach to obeying God's will. It covers almost all the problems that a believer might face and offers a rule for every circumstance. Certain religious groups in the Hebrew community during Jesus' time tried to live by these codes, making them a daily discipline. The Essenes and the Pharisees are two examples. Within the Christian tradition, many splinter groups have adopted a similar approach to their devotion. Puritanism, one of the founding religious cultures, was largely informed by a similar legalist approach to rules.

Before dismissing legalism out of hand, as the present generation has been prone to do, one must explore its strength. Surely there is need in life for some guiding principles, for a code of behaviour. Without order, and even in spite of it, human civilization descends into chaotic misery. Having laws at the very least establishes a code of principles to which people are accountable. The heart that longs to live a virtuous life quite naturally searches out the principles that are most likely to lead to truth and goodness. And who doesn't have doubts about their ultimate worthiness? Commandments help the frail and timid soul know, in a concrete way, when he or she has fulfilled God's will. In essence, I have no argument with law. It is an essential dimension of the faith journey. Only as it becomes rigid or gains an angry edge, becoming an end in itself, does it disrupt the eager and open soul.

What we loosely label as "fundamentalism" is a variation on the legalist approach to religion. In technical terms, Christian fundamentalism is the adherence to five foundational principles: the virgin birth, the inerrancy of Scripture, the premillennial return of Jesus, the substitutionary theory of the atonement, and the divinity of Christ. Five unbendable rules. Accept them as they are, or count yourself out of the fold. Besides its rigidity, I find this particular form of legalism to be too serious. Like the puritan impulse from which it grew, fundamentalism approaches itself and its own grasp at purity in much too rigorous a fashion. Donning a tight-fisted sobriety, it is unable to allow life to spin freely. Perhaps it is more precise to argue that legalism is a psychological state of mind, a fearful rigidity that seeks, above all else, to stay in control. One broken rule, one line overstepped, and the entire edifice of faith collapses. Hence, there is a distrust of the deeper passions—love, the erotic, pleasure, and happiness.

Heir to the hyper-Lutheranism or Calvinism that saw all human desires as base and impure, the right wing of Protestantism uses rules almost as an antidote to pleasure. We are all worms five feet high, according to Luther, and there is no good in us. Rules guard us from thinking too much about the bodily distractions that make us so base. Consequently, the North American puritan and/or fundamentalist ethos wards off sweeping emotions, fearing they might take over. Caught by a

GOD HATES RELIGION

rigid frame of mind, the devout ask, "Would we not be bound for perpetual enslavement if we allowed these dark passions to surface? We cannot or, to put it more succinctly, dare not dance."

Of course, this is a caricature, but, like a sour aftertaste, the influence of our puritan heritage still lingers, even in the more liberal Protestant denominations of North America. We dismiss the charges of legalism, but its fearful, "tight" tone still echoes in our hallowed halls. To touch its pulse, let's ask a few questions: Would we drink alcohol in our church? Wine or champagne are widely used as celebrative mixtures in society, but who would dare bring these beverages into a house of God for a party? How about dance? When was the last time we danced with all our might, as David did (2 Sam. 6:14), to show glory to God and experience the exhilaration of physical movement? We Christians are still frightened of our bodies and their uncontrolled ecstasy.

Perhaps there is a deeper fear here. The legalist approach to life fends off something more frightening than physical pleasure: the foreboding sense of ambiguity. Human existence is fraught with change and compromise. It is never as one-dimensional as we imagine. Legalism is a bolster to doubt, to the unsettling anxiety that human existence has no lasting meaning.

While the devout who keep the law seem to have a secure grasp of scriptural decrees, legalism falls short precisely because it is unable to appreciate the dialectical quality of truth as portrayed in Scripture. It ignores the obvious contradictions in biblical injunctions, and fails to face the yes and no quality of scriptural imperatives, a quality that captures the ambiguity of the human conditions of power and powerlessness.

Finally, legalism falls short as an interpretative method for it is of no use when we are faced with a situation for which there is no corresponding law. Where do we turn then? For instance, what law does the Bible set out for genetic medicine and research? It is similarly silent on the subject of nuclear war, abortion, and many other complex modern issues. If it's not mentioned, how do we find the rules? In essence, legalism is an

120

assault on the eternal, trying to possess "the truth." It has the prideful pretence to assume that this captivity of truth can be accomplished through human hands.

Situationalism and the Sliding Scale of Truth

On the opposite end of the spectrum from the legalist reading of Scripture is a situationalist or antinomian reading. Coming from the Latin word *nomos* meaning "law," antinomian suggests that there is no fixed or eternal rule that is binding for believers. Each new situation must be viewed as if for the first time, and appropriate rules must be designed according to the circumstances. Some liberal churches fall into the dismaying complexity of antinomianism. I often hear the criticism that liberals don't believe anything anymore.

The weakness in situationalism is exactly the opposite of legalism. If there are no lasting laws and nothing beyond human judgement in each successive situation, how do we avoid subjectivity? Won't the human will to power easily subvert the establishment of justice and right decision making? Law becomes a matter of personal choice, and any governing body of rules is subsumed under the authority of the individual to protect his or her "rights" or privileges. In these circumstances, justice is a question of power rather than righteousness, a matter of who has the most guns.

Moreover, there is no fixed doctrine to which one can call people to account or in which people can find security. Antinomianism assumes that the eternal can never be fixed. If legalism falls prey to the sin of pride, assuming too much for itself, situationalism is a victim of sloth, believing that there is nothing unique in the human situation that speaks of the divine or reflects, however weakly, the promise of the eternal.

There is an alternative to both the legalist and the antinomian approaches to rules and regulations. Focusing on biblical principles, we can follow an approach that the ministry of Jesus seems to maintain: contextuality. This involves the development of

GOD HATES RELIGION

some general principles originating in the Bible itself. These principles will help us to read scriptural injunctions and make ethical decisions in our daily lives.

In order to undertake this contextual reading of the Word of God, we will need to explore some of the major contextual paradigms within which the original laws were made. How did the ancients begin to order their world? What were their basic fears and hopes?

The Context of Property, Purity, and Piety

It is difficult for most North American Christian believers to comprehend that the major paradigms of Jesus' world were different from our own. While rules in our Western world focus on individual freedoms, material property rights, sexual indiscretions, and offences against one's physical person, Jesus' Palestine had other concerns. Their primary categories were honour and shame, patron and client, ownership and powerlessness, and purity and impurity. What we often deem immoral on sexual grounds is actually an issue of property in the Hebrew Scriptures. The ancient world was worried by the influence of outside culture, idolatry, and the breakdown of collectivity and the tribe; modern society has little concern over idol worship.

The commandment against adultery is a good example of the difference between the cultural paradigms. The seventh commandment did not argue against multiple sexual partners and the pursuit of wanton pleasure, as our modern world might see it. Adultery was a question of property rights. David, for instance, had many wives, according to 2 Samuel 12. Taking Bathsheba was considered adultery because he took another man's property. That was the sin. Nathan's story to David indicates that his wrongdoing was in robbing another person of his prized possession, and not David's infidelity to other sexual partners or wives.

Even when the actual acts being condemned are quite evident in the Bible, it remains a complex task to determine the motivations behind certain laws. Moreover, it is difficult to understand how certain rules were actually lived out in daily existence. We know that there was some effort to institutionalize the jubilee economic practices of Deuteronomy 15, but how these laws were played out in small town life is difficult to determine.

Certainly, we must be aware of the possibility of other determining factors in our examination of any law or regulation. We must be aware of the issues that made the law necessary, even though we might consider them irrelevant. Therefore caution, flexibility, and humility are the marks of any honest and open reflection on biblical rules.

Apocalypticism: Special Times Require Special Rules

It is essential to recall Jesus' central vision, and what he did with rules and regulations, before developing a contextual approach to biblical commandments. What was the focus of his ministry? While certainty is impossible, I believe Jesus' mission was to create an egalitarian community. He was unwilling to accept the role of patron over this community, and he asked his followers to refuse it as well. In servanthood and radical vulnerability, they were to live out a reign of God where justice and grace, forgiveness and acceptance, were everyone's birthright. In this circle, false barriers of status or privilege were torn down. In Christ, there were no distinctions.

If his intention was to create an egalitarian community fit for God's reign, then how does that affect the rules? Quite obviously those regulations that establish a hierarchy of righteousness were inappropriate and needed some translation. Or if they were unable to be transformed, they had to be rejected. Jesus often did this in the case of restrictions regarding leprosy, people who were touching bodily fluids, or those who were in contact with foreigners.

Another factor in the ministry of Jesus that might have influenced his understanding of the law was the imminence of the coming reign of God. If it was coming soon (the clear message of

GOD HATES RELIGION

John the Baptist and initially, at least, the thinking of Jesus himself), then some rules were counter-productive. They were cumbersome, taking up too much time and energy for a people preparing for the soon-to-arrive rule of God. All human activity was measured by the yardstick of apocalyptic urgency, and it coloured much of Christ's vision.

The implicit apocalypticism of Jesus' ministry that informs his understanding of many biblical regulations is illustrated in the following story of Sabbath regulations. Although it is found in all three Synoptic Gospels, we may have only one real attestation to the historicity of the story since Mark's version was most likely repeated by both Luke and Matthew.

It so happened that he was walking along through the grainfields on the sabbath day, and his disciples began to strip heads of grain as they walked along. And the Pharisees started to argue with him: "See here, why are they doing what's not permitted on the sabbath day?"

And he says to them: "Haven't you ever read what David did when he found it necessary, when both he and his companions were hungry? He went into the house of God, when Abiathar was high priest, and ate the consecrated bread, and even gave some to his men to eat. No one is permitted to eat this bread, except the priests!"

And he continued:

The sabbath day was created for Adam and Eve, not Adam and Eve for the sabbath day.

So, the son of Adam lords it even over the sabbath day (Mark 2:23-28, SV).

There is every likelihood that the final aphorism, "The sabbath day was created for Adam and Eve, not Adam and Eve for the sabbath day," has some merit as a historically factual rendition of a saying of Jesus. It is an easy-off-the-tongue saying, one readily memorized and well suited to the oral transmission of the period between Jesus' death and the actual writing of the first testaments. While the rest of the passage fits well into the post-resurrection debate between Jewish Christians and gentile Christians about the keeping of certain biblical laws, there is a continuity between this passage and the general attitude of Jesus to all the laws (see Matt. 5,6).

According to the law found in Deuteronomy 5:14 and Exodus 20:10, people were forbidden to work on the Sabbath day. In Deuteronomy, this injunction is linked to the fact that the people of Israel were slaves in Egypt. The rationale for the law was that everyone deserves a rest, even slaves. Keeping the Sabbath was a question of justice and obedience to God's reign of shalom. On the other hand, the Exodus injunction compares the Sabbath day with the rest God took after creating the earth. Resting was a re-enactment of that "holy" rest, an act of devotion and spiritual revitalization of the mundane order. It's a day when you say "enough is sufficient."

Since the Bible offers two distinct reasons for the same rule, the complexity of endeavouring to keep the Bible's laws is obvious. At the point of interpretation, our keeping of the Sabbath will differ depending on which reason we accept as supreme.

During the time of Jesus, the complexity of Sabbath laws was impressive. As often happens, the devoted assumed that righteousness is found in more, rather than fewer, rules. Believers were restricted from travel, work, and eating. It is possible that walking through grain fields would be considered by some legalists as a breach of Deuteronomic regulations, which stipulate that believers can't travel more than 2,000 cubits (3,600 yards) from their homes or a synagogue. On the other hand, it is more likely that the disciples' grinding of the ears of corn was construed as work, as the preparation of food forbidden by law. In either case, there was already enough criticism of the ministry of Jesus by religious authorities for him to catch more.

Jesus recognizes that, while the Sabbath law was established for good reasons, either to give justice to people or to preserve holiness within creation, even this central commandment may

GOD HATES RELIGION

be overturned or ignored in times of crisis. He employs the case of David, found in 1 Samuel 21:1-7, who, when his men were hungry, took the sacred Sabbath bread (see Lev. 24:1-9) prepared specifically for the high priests. Jesus is pointing out that King David himself, the greatest Israelite leader, broke Sabbath rules in emergencies. Given the circumstances, it was acceptable in God's sight. Jesus is claiming the same for his own ministry. To those who criticized his flouting of the law, he says, "These are special, drastic times, which require drastic measures. Surely our rules are not intended to impede God's reign, but to serve it."

It is a very tricky argument, but one that is central to the message of the Scriptures. No rules are eternal. They derive their authority from God's love and peace and justice. The prophet Micah is quite clear about this. God does not expect ritual cleanliness or mountainous offerings, but justice and mercy (Mic. 6:8). Jesus is arguing that law is not heteronomous (imposed from outside) or autonomous (imposed from within), but thenomous (by the authority of God). Hence, it must be constantly tested against the will of God.

The leader from Galilee judged that his ministry was of utmost importance. Since it heralded the coming of the reign of God, other biblical rules were secondary. Elsewhere, Jesus is portrayed as keeping the Sabbath law. Luke 4:16 portrays him as a devout Jew, following Sabbath rules by going to synagogue in his hometown of Nazareth. Obviously, the story of breaking Sabbath regulations indicates that, for Jesus, the proximity and urgency of the coming reign was a determinative factor that dictated whether the laws applied.

The coming reign was marked by an open table fellowship, as already stated, where there are no distinctions drawn between pure and impure and the respectable and despised sit side by side. Clearly, the first Christian tables had this quality. Paul's injunctions in the first letter to the church in Corinth were to correct the distortions of table fellowship and to reaffirm the egalitarian, non-hierarchical dimensions of the communion

126

meal. The apocalyptic mission was further extended in the Jesus movement as it sought to establish a non-brokered society, one growing from a grassroots egalitarianism.

If there are those who need rules to live by, these apocalyptic principles of spiritual and social egalitarianism are good places to begin. They can guide one's reading of Scripture and may well be suitable for determining ethical decision making.

An Antidote to Legalism

I would suggest that the apocalyptic fervour of the Jesus movement is an appropriate base upon which to found a new company of the Messiah. Imagine what worship would become if it began with a simple meal, one open to all and any. If we cleared away all the furniture in the sanctuary except a single table (not unlike those first church settings), a table at which there is room for everyone. If everyone were invited, rich and poor, prestigious and unknown alike. If at that meal, there were bread, daily bread, just enough. Everyone would have enough. In that company there would be no one more important than others, no one too lowly or mean to be included. The mark of leadership would be servanthood.

It may sound idealistic, perhaps impractical, but it is precisely this vision that continues to break out of the Christian community. Whenever there are reforms, this primary egalitarian focus re-emerges. This radical community is the antidote to the raging religious fundamentalism that often passes for spiritual zeal in our context.

Chapter 9

Retributive Transcendence meets Extravagant Immanence

You cannot reach God by the work of right thinking or by a sacrifice of the intellect or by submission to strange authorities such as the doctrines of the church and the Bible.

—Paul Tillich 1948, xv

The Problem of Prayer

Let us once again imagine our way into the sacred space surrounding us, as we did at the beginning of chapter 8. We've been sitting in the pew, but now it's time to step behind the table at the front of the sanctuary. At this altar, so called by certain segments of the tradition, we gather up all the mixed and multiple yearnings of the community and call upon the Creator of the Universe. To this table we bring our burdens, questions, anxieties, doubts, hopes, and fears and lay them down before the Maker of all things. From this table we take a message of hope for the world made new. At least, that's the theory, but what does it mean to the troubled spirit?

As I prepare to pray from behind this table, I think of how often I have heard the pleading echoes of hushed complaints uttered by the hospital bed, at the kitchen table, or in the funeral parlour: "I prayed he would get better. I went to church and listened to everything they told me. The preacher said that if I prayed faithfully enough, God would give me a blessing. I'd get what I needed because God knows best. So I prayed that my husband would get better, that the cancer would go away. And it didn't. He died last night. So what went wrong? Heaven knows I needed my husband to live. Why did God turn away from me? What do I do when my prayers aren't answered?"

What do we do when our prayers go out to the Almighty and disappear into the good night? When we receive no response? We've tried hard to believe, to follow the commandments. Now, when we need God most, our laments are ignored.

We are at the heart of the matter, aren't we? There has never been a better rebuttal of the truth of religion than unanswered prayer. If God hates religion, it is because religion promises easy answers to prayers and there are none to be found. Any cynic, no matter what elegant arguments are put forth, can always fall back on the great silence. From the vantage point of this table at the front of the sanctuary, we can look about at all our religious trappings: the banners, pews, baptismal fonts, even our contrite hearts, all designed to please God. And still our doubt will ask: "If God is all loving and all powerful, then why is there pain, why is there suffering for those who are pure and largely innocent? Is God unable to intervene, hence not omnipotent, or perhaps just not all loving?" Is God an outdated myth, a throwback to primitive paranoia?

The obvious and perhaps most honest response to unanswered prayer is to admit that our faith is, in fact, a mistake. God is dead. The One to whom we're praying doesn't exist. Worship is a misguided hoax and prayer a cruel joke. Since there is no heavenly "Father," prayers will always go unanswered. Our lives are not governed by a benevolent, eternal power. On the contrary, we are pawns in an endless game of dice governed by the laws of probability. Some people die; some are cured. You pay your money and take your chances.

It sounds unduly harsh and crude, but this is a very faithful response, one I'm sure any sceptic, even the religious variety, would appreciate. Anger and the denial of God's existence do

GOD HATES RELIGION

have their spiritual place. For instance, in the Hebrew Scriptures there is the story of Job, an afflicted man who is constantly angry with God. He voices his objections to the spiritual "precepts" of his day with a bold openness that borders on a denial of God's very existence. His refreshing honesty is marvellous.

There is a story told of modern Jobs, Jewish prisoners in a Nazi concentration camp. Their suffering was so great that they gathered together to put God on trial for breaking the promises of the covenant. A make-shift court room was set up in the barracks and, bringing forth countless witnesses, they built their case. Families had been split up, children and babies had been thoughtlessly massacred, women were turned into prostitutes, and old men chained like dogs. The litany of suffering was endless. Darkness had won. There was no light of hope, love, or benevolence to be found in human existence. When the night came, the gathered company found God guilty as charged and condemned God to death. Then, as the sun set, it being the Sabbath, the entire community went out to pray.

There are indeed moments when life seems to have no reasonable pattern, when sickness prevails and justice does not. Who wouldn't curse the darkness? And yet, as those Jews in the concentration camp testify, anger and unbelief are worthy offerings to God, a gateway into the pain of our Creator.

Nevertheless, we are human beings and our frail, finite hearts search for more assurance. Hence, when anger does not satisfy us and our prayers are still unanswered, we are often tempted to let God off the hook. In desperation, we explain away God's silence, much like a child rationalizes a parent's unjust behaviour: "God is too busy to worry about me. Who am I, anyway? Just a small speck in the span of eternity. Why should I be surprised that my prayers are in vain? I haven't been consistent in my devotional life and Bible readings. Why should God pay attention to me when I have neglected my side?"

A more subtle form of rationalizing God's apparent indifference is the argument that the Almighty has other purposes for our lives, not yet understandable. So our prayers are not an-

RETRIBUTIVE TRANSCENDENCE MEETS EXTRAVAGANT IMMANENCE

swered because God gives us a response we are not anticipating. We cannot honestly expect God's reply to our pleadings to walk up to us with the label, "God's Answer to Prayer." We have to search for it, sometimes in strange places. And even if that search is in vain, we are called to persevere.

If we are unable to live a life of searching and questing, we introduce a misleading distortion into the debate on unanswered prayer. In an attempt to save God's righteousness in the face of unwarranted pain, we transform suffering into a positive event. The death of a beloved is construed as necessary: "God needed my little boy in heaven," or "God loved him so much that paradise was the only place for him. That's why God refused to listen to my cry." Of all the traditional responses to unanswered prayer, this one is the most obnoxious. God is transformed into a tyrant, an unfeeling, childish demi-god, while human suffering is systematically discounted.

Most deplorable of our responses to unanswered prayer, though, is the "It's not happening to me" approach. Here is a great self-inflicted hoax. We tell ourselves that indeed our prayers have been answered, and repeat it until we are convinced. Death is not a break or a separation—it's a gift. "Oh, it's better this way. He wouldn't have wanted to linger, a mercy, really. Now he's with Uncle Jack, Aunt Edna. Nothing is wrong. God answered our prayers, really." Whispered phrases at the funeral parlour, casket-side: "It's almost as if he's sleeping. Doesn't she look better? He's happier now; no more anguish. She would have preferred it this way."

Perhaps there are no satisfying answers for those whose prayers appear to be ignored by God. None. Maybe there are only great questions in human life, and our efforts should be expended in discovering what these might be. Our role in confronting the calamity of death or suffering is to remain faithful to our questions. Just as we stand by our friends through difficult, uncertain times, so we stand by our questions (Rilke), faithfully asking. And all the while we trust in a power beyond ourselves, hoping that someday we may live into our answers.

GOD HATES RELIGION

So our prayers, rather than being requests for answers, are really quests for the right questions. We are now teetering on the brink of a deep insight: perhaps prayer itself must be transformed.

We say to ourselves, "Oh, well. I must have been praying in the wrong way. God is not Santa Claus. We can't just draw up a wish list, hoping that because we've been 'good,' God will fill our stockings with marvellous toys. God doesn't work like that. My prayers go unanswered because I've misused prayer."

Here I find hope, the substance of a revitalized and radically refreshing approach to religion and God. Indeed, prayer is not drawing up a wish list. According to Douglas John Hall in *When You Pray*, it is an act by which we enter into God's world and believe our way into God's presence. It has a mysterious quality, one that the mind cannot fathom. Guided by the heart into the mysterious world beyond knowing and seeing, answers become irrelevant. Through prayer we seek only to be present to the eternal pulse that beats through all creation.

While this may be a good definition of prayer, it doesn't deal with the nagging question of innocent suffering, nor the injustices of human life. Surely this God with whom we commune, being all powerful, could do something to heal our pain. Unless, of course, God is *not* all powerful, at least not in the way we have traditionally thought.

The end of the twentieth century may be characterized as a decline and fall of our human concepts of God. Corresponding as they do to ambiguous finite concepts, our images of the divine may be in need of major renovations; they may be getting in the way rather than helping. Is it possible that God's essence does not consist of the manipulative power to change or alter human events, that God's love curtails God's capacity to act? Perhaps our Maker is not a detached deity controlling earth's affairs, eternally and dispassionately. As unorthodox as this reasoning may seem, there is good evidence that Jesus himself was attempting in a similar fashion to redirect the thinking about God that was crippling the people of his day.

132

Language about God

A brief digression into theological linguistic concerns is essential at this point. We must recognize that when human beings speak of God, they are using allegorical language. Apart from the possible exception of Moses, no historical character has ever claimed to have seen God. How then can we speak with any authority of this Being whom we claim is above understanding? Even in the case of inspired revelation, we must ask how our finite physiological and psychological paradigms can ever hope to grasp the true nature of the Creator of the universe.

Surely we are required to speak of God in images. Even our use of the word "God" posits certain ideas concerning this power or force or being with whom we commune. There is no language, no image, no gender, or salutation applied to the Maker of all things that is more credible or correct than any other. They are all trying to point to a mystery beyond language and human comprehension.

What we capture with our words is but a small fraction of what or who God is. Only those who are closed or foolish would claim to do more, since God is above any ideas, greater than our feeble phrases. For this reason, all God-language is allegorical, comparative speech.

One might well ask, If God is so far above our thoughts, how can we, with any assurance, speak of God at all? What's the point? Language about God is not so important as a means to describe the deity, as it is a way to name for believers what is important and eternal. The images and allegories we use for God betray who we are and what we feel is essential and lasting in life. For this reason we name God. In the naming, we sift through life's complexities and ambiguities to uncover some specks of truth for ourselves. God-talk is a mirror.

For example, if we sense that an all-pervading purpose in life is important, we will naturally portray God as the mainstay of a providential plan, as the guardian of a trustworthy order on this planet. On the other hand, if we feel that military prowess is essential for the smooth functioning of our civilization, then the war-like image of a heavenly Power will emerge. In our naming of God, we render sacred our most precious hopes and fears.

The point of this digression is to illustrate that all God-talk is conditioned and contextual. It is neither right nor wrong, for it seeks to capture the yearning of the specific context in which it is spoken. Therefore, if you have trouble with the church because it claims to have certain strict codes or rules about how and in what context to address God, you are justified in your criticisms. God is greater than our categories, and it is only the very stubborn or frightened who resist the re-naming of God as human needs change.

The Parent God

Jesus himself was appreciative of the need to continue transforming the language about God. He employed many images to describe God: father, mother, hen, king, vineyard owner, to name but a few. It's a typical chicken-or-the-egg question whether the images of God proposed by Jesus emerged from his understanding of heaven's rule coming to earth or if his picture of God's immanent reign emerged from a radically subversive image of God. It's essentially not important which came first. They fit together well.

Jesus did not speak of God as a Mighty Being who marshalled the heavenly hosts. Nor did he suggest that God was a distant, eternal Judge. Relying more on the prophetic tradition that personalized the relationship between God and human beings (see Hosea), Jesus imagined God as a close relative, an intimate associate, a parent. In a sensational stroke, one which still takes my breath away, Jesus gave special intimacy to his language about his Maker. Using the Aramaic word *abba*, he portrayed God as close and playfully intimate, a "daddy."

There is more to this image than the Father and/or parent paradigm, though that is rich soil indeed. Listen to the explanation Jesus gives to his disciples about prayer and you will catch the flavour of this new image of God. In the First Gospel, it reads:

And when you pray, don't act like phonies. They love to stand up and pray in houses of worship and on street corners, so they can show off in public. I swear to you, their prayers have been answered! When you pray, go into a room by yourself and shut the door behind you. Then pray to your Father, the hidden one. And your Father, with his eye for the hidden, will applaud you. And when you pray, you should not babble on as the pagans do. They imagine that the length of their prayers will command attention. So don't imitate them. After all, your Father knows what you need before you ask. Instead you should pray like this:

Our Father in the heavens,
your name be revered.
Impose your imperial rule,
enact your will on earth as you have in heaven.
Provide us with the bread we need for the day.
Forgive our debts
to the extent that we have forgiven those in debt to us.
And please don't subject us to test after test,
but rescue us from the evil one (Matt. 6:5-15, SV).

God Is Hidden, Close and Caring

As Jesus speaks of the Maker of the Universe, ironically there is a refreshing down-to-earth quality that surrounds his "Father in the heavens." Rather than the distant watch-maker God of Genesis, or the warrior king of Exodus, Jesus speaks of a God who is close, one who is not impressed with the show of religion and the posturing of piety. This God is too intimate with the pathways of the heart to be fooled by outward trappings and vacuous displays of devotion. This God is found, or perhaps it is more accurate to say we are found by this God, in the dark recesses, in hidden places. Eternity is visible only as we drop

GOD HATES RELIGION

our pretence of seeing it. Whether we are alone or in a circle, prayer is being who we truly are, relinquishing our boasting and our cowering. Then God appears.

The God of the Lord's Prayer knows us even better than we know ourselves. In God's eyes, we are like offspring, needing bread, protection, and comfort. In Jesus' prayer, I can find no conditions, no pre-requisites for God's loving presence. God is and God gives. We are asked only to be who we are, to accept in humility that we are created beings, to rejoice in our creature-hood and accept openly that we need the help and assurance of a Creator.

Of course, if God is a parent, then God knows the suffering and vulnerability of creating children. If we love them, we must let them be free; once they are separated from us, we become weak. The creator is at the mercy of the beloved. Imagine yourself as a parent. Is it not an invitation into pain and heart ache? Along with the exhilaration of watching new life in our children are the hardships of being the brunt of their wars of independence, the soul mate in their disappointments and broken dreams. Is there a greater weakness and powerlessness than that of creating living beings? For, in the final analysis, we are captive to whatever they might do with the gift of life we have given them.

It is possible that the Creator of all knows this suffering eternally. If so, what does that say of God? Is it possible that God's power is shaped or at least influenced by the weakness of love and creating?

God Is Not Achieved

What is clearly implied in the prayer of Jesus and in his advice about praying is that God is not a stone deity. God is not an idol that demands sacrifice and must be goaded into action by a mountain of prayers.

During the drought of the 1930s, farmers in western Canada were losing their livestock at alarming rates. Farmyards were

RETRIBUTIVE TRANSCENDENCE MEETS EXTRAVAGANT IMMANENCE

literally filled with the carcasses of dying animals. There was not enough water for the people, let alone the cattle. Into this desperate situation came a young and zealous theological student. It was his summer job to visit these farms and offer what pastoral support he could. At one sheep ranch, he bounded up the steps of the house to pay his pastoral visit and, upon encountering the curiously tongue-tied farmer, suggested they go inside for prayers. "Surely God will not ignore the pleas of a righteous man," said the practicing pastor.

The farmer was unmoved for a moment, looking off to a hazy horizon. Then, sensing the untried eagerness of his visitor, he agreed. "I'll come and pray with you, but first come and visit my sheep." So the pair walked out into the pasture by the homestead. There, they found dozens of sheep, bleating for water and dying because there was none to be found. In the midst of the moaning and anguish of his sheep, the farmer turned to the student and said, "Now, pastor, if you can pray better than those sheep, you go right ahead."

Long, pretentious sentences and eternally pious petitions will not be regarded with any special attention by the God of Jesus. God is not achieved or assaulted like some detached monarch. There are no conditions separating us from God. Jesus was arguing in his time, as did the reformers in the sixteenth century, that you cannot reach God through right thinking or by submitting to a specific article of dogma or doctrine of law. There are no authorities separating us from God, for God is as close as our tears and our groaning.

There is a divine extravagance here, which is vital. It is absolutely central to the hope of those who are lost, and usually embarrassing to those who think themselves pious. God's love is not held back as punishment or stored up for those who know the secret key to heaven. It is lavished on every living being. Jesus makes it clear that each one of us is to have daily bread, simply for the asking. There is no stipulation that we must deserve it or earn it in some fashion. God gives. Full stop. A miraculous mystery. Nevertheless, love is not a simple emotion,

137

as anyone can attest. It is often a paradoxical sensation, a bag of contradictory feelings. To say that God is love is to construct more, rather than fewer, layers of interpretation on the divine.

There is no final or lasting response to this question of God-talk, to imaging God. Each generation will have to re-develop its picture of the God who created all things. The Bible argues that God is not static, not a fixed Being, but a moving, changing, repenting, acting power. From Genesis to the book of Revelation, the Scriptures give testimony to a deity in flux, One who breathes life, storms at injustice, repents of rash judgement, shakes the earth, and moves to the beat of an eternal drum—the human heart.

Church: A Community of Foundlings

God is not detached or disinterested, but very close to the created order. If there is a dominant allegory of God, it is to portray God as one with whom we are in relation—not a foreign static principle, but a close friend or relative. The church that lives within the world of that intimate God knows itself to be found like some orphan on a step, taken into someone's care without having deserved or expected such compassion. We are a community of foundlings—without pretence of importance or piety; just a band of people with a need to be inspired and loved into what we might become.

Chapter 10

The Inverting Principle

Neither works of piety nor works of morality nor works of the intellect establish unity with God. They follow from this unity, but they do not make it.

—Tillich 1948, xv

Never-ending Guilt

The faithful are one with the agnostic doubter in at least one key respect: we all feel guilt. Whether we're devout or indifferent, no one escapes the primordial sense of deep "shoulds": I should be more loving; I should be more kind; I should give to the less fortunate.

As we stand at the front of the church we might perceive that this colossal building is built, to a certain extent, by guilt. Feeling culpable, people give money to memorial funds in the name of relatives they should have loved more dearly. It is guilt that adds the zeros onto so many cheques destined for the construction of the new organ and the paint job on the ceiling.

Is the church the house that guilt built? Of course, that question is an exaggeration, but guilt has been a strong influence, especially in the Protestant tradition. Generations of clergy have spent their life's blood adoring and bolstering a great Parent God in the sky. This God's sole purpose seems to be to make us feel culpable when we can't achieve the impossible standards laid out in the law.

GOD HATES RELIGION

John Calvin, the great founder of the reformed Protestant tradition, once said that much Christian preaching and teaching was like holding an ostrich egg up to a bunch of bantam hens and saying, "Do your best." Who can escape the sense of falling short?

In a social context where the rules have been consistently sliding towards leniency, everyone has twinges of guilt. It's like a virus in the air we breathe. No one, not even little children, has antibodies to fight it off. The question is: What do you do with your guilt? Where does it go? What do you do with all the accumulated "shoulds" of a lifetime? "I should have kept in touch with my school mates; I should have been polite to my mother last week; I should have gone to the hospital to visit that dear, sick relative; I should spend more quality time with the children." Should is stacked upon shoulds, and what do we do? Some people pack their guilt in neat parcels, juggling them through life's doorways, thinking it's the normal burden you bear when you become an adult. Once out of infancy, you start to accumulate these guilt boxes. And it all seems natural enough—growing up is guilting up.

Heaven knows the world is filled with people who delight in passing out guilt gifts for anyone vulnerable or gullible enough to take them. It's easy. Put on that parental condescending aura, tie a neat ribbon around your question, and say: "Do you really think you should be doing that?" or "Have you forgotten something?" or "You mustn't be naughty!" The surprising thing is that we actually accept these guilt packs, undismayed by our culpability quotient.

If you don't carry it about, you can bury your guilt in a deep psychic pit and pretend it's not there. "Who me? Guilty? Not on your life!" That's what we say to ourselves while digging the mental grave for our guilt. To protect a fragile exterior people construct an inner black hole and dump into it all the unwanted criticisms, the missed opportunities, and broken promises—hurtful, guilt-ridden memories. Unfortunately, guilt is not bio-degradable. If you bury it, it doesn't go away. It stays where you

THE INVERTING PRINCIPLE

left it, waiting for just the right crisis in order to spring free and pollute your soul's ecological balance.

Some sadly misguided individuals like to transfer their guilt, as if it were an emotional version of household waste. It's a natural enough reaction. After all, most guilt is messy, so who would want it lying around the living room? Give it to someone else to handle. That's the solution. These guilt exchangers delight in blaming everyone else for their problems. "It's not my fault! Someone else is to blame!" Convenient slogans. Whether the criticism is warranted or not, the guilt is then transferred onto a usually unsuspecting third party.

Finally, there's the ultimate attitude towards guilt. We wallow in it and exult in some rather heavy duty self-pity. Get down and grovel! Let's immobilize ourselves with guilt-initiated self-doubt! Parking our soul at the office of emotional suicide, we book ourselves out of living and never have to come up for air. If these approaches to guilt prove unsatisfactory, I can suggest another option. How about learning to avoid it altogether by being responsible?

In many ways, guilt is an addictive and destructive spiritual trap. Here's how it works. Imagine that our emotions are like a car; guilt is the brake pedal and responsibility is the accelerator. Note that they're very close together. First, we do something hurtful, a harsh word, a deliberate act of abuse. Or we forget to do something helpful, send a card, play with our child. It isn't long before there's a tingling in our spirit; something is wrong, and we're involved.

Given the religious perversity of the North American soul, our automatic reaction is to hit the brake. Put a stop to the "bad" behaviour. We scold ourselves, saying: "I'm a rotten person. I shouldn't be so evil. Do I ever feel guilty." Of course, the problem is that guilty feelings don't move us anywhere. In fact, they're an obstacle to travelling beyond the very actions we deplore. Sometimes we mistakenly feel that guilt will help us, perhaps direct and strengthen our efforts to make amends and get us out of our jam. But just as the brakes on a car only serve to

141

GOD HATES RELIGION

keep the car where it is, guilt doesn't create anything but immo-
bility and more guilt. It's a trap.

I often wonder if we don't feel guilty because, in reality, we
don't want to move ahead. In a twisted way, guilt is a self-
inflicted punishment for doing what we want to do even though
we know it's hurtful. Rather than resorting to healthy behaviour
that would require some frightening and uncomfortable change,
we stick with the harmful habits, paying for our "indiscretions"
with the pain of guilt. The ultimate question is: Do we want to
be well? The next time you feel guilty, ask yourself if you want
to be free of it. If you do, and that's a big "if," take your foot off
the brake and press the accelerator of responsibility. Now you
can go forward.

Unlike guilt, responsibility is the acceptance that, yes, we
have been involved in a wrongful act or event, and, yes, we are
also free to live differently. Sure, we feel regret or remorse, but
above all we recognize that in every fresh moment, in every new
sunrise, there is an opportunity to change our attitude and our
lifestyle. Human beings are not pre-programmed. We can make
amends. We are more than our faults and there is nothing
stopping us from taking this day or this week and addressing
those actions or events that previously caused us pain.

We must pause to reflect for a moment, since there's one
catch: we have to know ourselves to be forgiven. Can we look in
the mirror, see all the wrinkles and warts, and still proclaim that
we are forgiven and loveable? If the Gospels testify to anything,
it is the love of a forgiving Creator God who has forgiven us
before we ask.

It is precisely at this point that I know my life is a communal
affair. Forgiveness requires company, someone outside of myself. It starts most easily when I forgive another. Then they can
forgive me in turn and together we can forgive others. Eventually it becomes a group event, with the whole circle practicing
tolerance and patience with each other. Only as I forgive am I
forgiven, and only as I am forgiven can I forgive. Call it a
spiritual cycle.

The Inverting Gospel

The gospel record contains an unsettling message, one which undermines every principle of "established" institutional religion. It runs contrary to the heavenly parent image of God and undercuts the omnipresent message of guilt. The message is this: Guilt is not what God expects or wants. God does not begin with "shoulds."

On the contrary, God is the one who begins the cycle of forgiving. It was and is God's initial gift. Life, love, and forgiveness are the initial gifts that make possible the forgiveness of others. God's giving undermines all the religious structures that would mask or denigrate the essential "giftedness," the extravagance of God's love.

The gospels are a testimony to this basic, unsettling, and liberating message of God's giving and forgiving. Call it the inverting principle of the Holy Scriptures. Up to this point, I have hinted at this principle and nibbled at the edges. Now it is time to hit the nail on the head, so to speak. The "good news," the central gospel conviction, is that love stems from being loved.

Now I suggest we all take a walk in the park with that phrase ringing in our hearts. Love stems from being loved. It cannot be programmed by thundering morality or invasive guilt or wearing-out-the-knees piety. Not even God can make you love. Your devotion to and faith in God are derivative of the devotion and faith already shown by the Maker and made manifest in the created order. Love, all human love, proceeds from the love we have been shown through the cycle of life and death.

An Infant's Perspective

Let us begin with birth. It is the touch and tenderness of a mother that transmits the vital message of life and love to an infant. Christ said we had to become as a child to enter the reign of God, so here's an exercise. Take a few quiet moments, relax in

GOD HATES RELIGION

your favourite chair, and imagine yourself as a baby. Picture yourself once again in your mother's arms. What do you know about anything? What are the lessons you can learn from that perspective?

First, think about life itself, what a gift it is. As babies, I don't suspect we give it much thought. Life just is. Who needs to distinguish what's living and what's not? From our perspective, it's all in all. Isn't that good? Glass marbles, juice in a bottle, the stuffed toy by the fireplace, they're all alive. We try to hang on to that thinking as long as possible, but "mature" people will want to persuade us that some things are not living creatures. They will tell us that rocks, trees, sky, balloons, candle light are "inanimate objects." (That means they don't have a soul.) Why do we believe these "wise ones"? They have forgotten what we, as babies, know to be true. Everything is living, all objects of this miraculous world have a unique rhythm—a part in the never-ending melody. No matter how slowly they move, all things on the planet live.

As infants, we probably haven't yet made the chief mistake of living: separating our living from the living of the things around us. Our tongue, the blanket, our father's beard; these are all connected. There's no division, no distinction. Again, those who call themselves elders will try to dissuade us from such reasoning, suggesting instead that our life is discreet and distinct, unattached to other living beings. Don't give in—they're too old and crusty to realize how life joins to life. Moreover, the world is in a great mess right now precisely because they ignored what we, as babies, can feel so strongly. All life is connected.

Besides life, there's something warm, something that is not the blanket, the beard, or the bed. It's there but we haven't been able to touch it yet. Call it a very strong yearning, not for food really, though it is a similar feeling. It's the longing for closeness, for the sense of oneness with our mother when she feeds us. It flickers in the eyes of the other large faces that drift into our line of vision. What is it, that deep desire? We name this delicious, comforting sensation "love."

144

THE INVERTING PRINCIPLE

We're just picking up the prime directive. We human beings are first and foremost lovers. We reach out to join ourselves with others around us. As infants, we love instinctively, but as we mature, let's never forget to allow ourselves to love. Don't shy away from it even though it may gain frightening undertones, the bedevilling cross-currents of rejection and betrayal. There are some who have decided that love is overrated, an unworthy enterprise. They think hate and greed and prejudice are more trustworthy and self-satisfying. Resist them. Of all the joys of living, love is the only medicine for the sickness of the broken heart.

Finally, there's laughter, an underrated principle of this God-given order. Besides love, laughter is one of the simplest yet miraculous feats we humans can accomplish. Believe me, as infants it even beats chewing on our toes. We've already begun to build up a storehouse of laughter. At present, we're smiling. Oh yes, the sceptical ones may say it's just gas, but we know better. We're curling up our mouths, our eyes are dancing because we feel good. Good! It's a beginning. Soon we will start to make noises as we smile. Then our tummies will jiggle, our lips will flap. Those things at the end of our shoulders (we call them arms) will move all around. For the moment, time stands still. That's laughter and there's nothing like it. Of all human acts, it is the most magical. It melts hardness, banishes fear, joins hearts, and even reaches beyond the mystery of birth and death to restore hope. We could call laughter the medicine of immortality.

So there they are, life, love, and laughter. Even as infants, we know them as fundamental lessons of living. The whole created order exudes life, love, and laughter and we are able to love and laugh precisely because we have received so much in the first place. There is a principle of reciprocity built into creation. On the basis of God's love, we are able to love. It can never be forced or coerced. All authentic spiritual authority is based on this unsolicited outpouring of love; any other ordering is false and eventually destructive.

GOD HATES RELIGION

The Troubled Question

How do we structure a community of believers on the inverting principle, the dynamic of unsolicited love? At the beginning of the Jesus movement, once it was clear that the Master was not returning immediately, there were conflicting views on how the establishment of a church or a community of believers should be structured. There were obviously several options to follow and none had any more authority than another. Some disciples favoured a traditional hierarchical model that mirrored the structure of temple worship and required priests and presiders. This group might well be represented by Peter and the twelve in Jerusalem.

A second option for the structuring of a religious organization followed the scholarly, aesthetic route. There were plenty of examples to model one's life after: the Essenes, certain sects of Zealots, desert hermits, and prophets like John the Baptist. Whoever was able to piece together the scholastic material that formed the basis for much of Matthew and Luke's work may well have had this form of church in mind. (See Crossan 1991, 1995 for further details.) Another option was one that mirrored the ministry of Jesus, the itinerant, seemingly boundless, wandering of a wise man. The two-by-two commission represents this third possible order for the Christian community.

The following text falls within the great debate around structure, but it also cuts much deeper, to the very heart of the religious enterprise. The disciples have been fighting, arguing with each other, and Jesus calls them aside.

> *And they came to Capernaum. When he got home, he started questioning them, "What were you arguing about on the road?" They fell completely silent, because on the road they had been bickering about who was the greatest.*
>
> *He sat down and called the twelve and says to them, "If any of you wants to be 'number one,' you have to be last of all and servant of all!"*

146

THE INVERTING PRINCIPLE

And he took a child and had her stand in front of them, and he put his arm around her, and he said to them, "Whoever accepts a child like this in my name is accepting me. And whoever accepts me is not so much accepting me as the one who sent me" (Mark 9:33-37, SV).

This is a simple story, all too often employed to engender guilt and submissiveness among the powerless. The tyranny of self-seeking servanthood was disguised as virtue and imposed on those who could not resist. But, going beyond the damaging use of this image to the story itself, we discover that there is an example contained within this parable (see also Mark 3:31-35; 8:34-37; John 13:12-17) of the reverse thinking that characterized the ministry of Jesus. Those who would be disciples of Jesus will begin in the most unlikely place, not as leaders but as servants.

The use of a child as paradigmatic of God's coming reign captures the heartbeat of Christ's message. Apart from their innocence and diminutive size, children represent the forgotten, the lost and helpless, the vulnerable nobodies, in Crossan's words, of that age. A female child was worth even less than a male child. She was little more than a piece of property and would not be considered valuable until her child-bearing years. All children were ignored until they reached maturity. These nobodies, these less-than-legal entities, are the symbol of Jesus' reign on earth. In his time, this would have been a disturbing picture, one that I suspect is still viewed with suspicion.

What if the kingdom of "nobodies" is the dominant symbol of Christ's company? While this is a helpful idea, I would expand it and argue that it is a company of people who cannot achieve salvation on their own. They are helpless and utterly unable to find their own righteous status as long as they try to "go it alone." Faith requires company, a sustaining and refreshing interchange of love.

147

GOD HATES RELIGION

The Church: Always Undermining

If lasting faith needs a circle of people who give love to each other and who all receive love from a source outside themselves, then "true religion" is always undermining or subverting itself. If the love that makes faith possible cannot be controlled or forced, then any pattern will be constantly shifting. There can be no structured ordering of what is, by its very nature, unorderable. The gift is given. The pretence to earn the gift, possess it, or take it by storm, is false. God gives. End of argument.

Chapter 11

Safe Church or Risking Church?

Cheap grace is the deadly enemy of our Church. We are fighting today for costly grace.... Cheap grace means the justification of sin without the justification of the sinner. Grace alone does everything, they say, and so everything can remain as it was before.... Cheap grace is given without discipleship, grace without the cross, grace without Jesus Christ, living and incarnate.

—Bonhoeffer 1959, 35

A Holy Hole

Is there any real point to religion? Is there any substance at its core? In response to our doubts, I offer a wonderful tale of how faith-filled people can risk a great deal for the sake of a great dream. There is no better standard of the church's value than its willingness to risk even its own survival for the sake of a wider mission. All my rational arguments aside, the community of faith is essentially that band of people joined by trust in the dream of the world as it could be.

Alberta is a relatively young province in Canada. It was settled in the late nineteenth century and many of its honoured institutions date back to that time. This is the story of how one of those institutions, the University of Alberta, found its home.

Just after the turn of the century, when the town of Edmonton stood on the north side of the North Saskatchewan river and the scattered houses in the hamlet of Strathcona were about all there

GOD HATES RELIGION

was on the south side, a dream began to form. A university. Why not create a western centre of scholarship, able to prepare students for the great, modern world that was unfolding?

The legislature of the newly founded province, based in Edmonton, became the locus of the cantankerous debate over the university's location. Where was its proper home? A strong contingent, spear-headed by a law firm whose partners would later become prime ministers and premiers, argued that the university had to be based in the south. Calgary was the obvious choice. Mr. Rutherford, the founder of the university, was the champion for Edmonton. From his home on the southern banks of the river, he looked out from his back windows and saw a great institution rising. While it was quite visible to him, there wasn't much out there for anyone else to see but a few prairie-grass-fringed streets and lots of scrub forest.

Then some Methodists with a similar dream bought a parcel of land near Rutherford House. Desirous of having an institution dedicated to the search for truth, and led by an industrious principal, these believers cut their way through the alders to find a suitable building site for a theological college. They came from the community of believers who had already built Alberta College (a high school for rural teens) on the north side of the river. Before the great debate over a university site was even close to its conclusion, before the province had even formally decided to build one, the visionaries dug a hole in the ground on the south side of the river and announced that they were going to build a men's residence to house an incredible number of students for that time, one hundred no less.

For a while, there was only an empty hole in the ground. Some thought the Methodists had finally overstepped their common sense: "Silly for people to be so rash." Others quietly laughed up their sleeves. Rutherford, on the other hand, was declaring to anyone who would listen that the south side of the river near Strathcona was the most obvious location for the university. "After all, the Methodists are building a huge college residence there. It would be perfect for housing university as

150

SAFE CHURCH OR RISKING CHURCH?

well as theological students."

And so it was. The University of Alberta, one of the largest institutions of higher learning in Canada, was located on its present site due in large part to some wild-eyed disciples of John Wesley who took a chance and dug a hole in the ground because of a vision they shared. This is a wonderfully true parable to guide the church in this age of crisis and change.

The Parable of the Talents

There is an ancient parable with a similar meaning, one most Christians recognize as the parable of the talents. To appreciate its message we have to recognize that meaning in life is a question of perspective. From the point of view of a turkey, Thanksgiving is a despicable celebration centred on the unsolicited forced feeding and subsequent mass slaughter of their race. From the vantage of dandelions, modern manicured lawns are a graveyard of lost hopes.

The Bible is no different. We read its stories and hear them as they correspond to our lived experience. Most of us hear the story of the prodigal son and think of our own indiscretions that have caused hurt in our inner circle. When the story of the good Samaritan is read, we imagine ourselves as the stranger who reaches out to a wounded sufferer by the side of the road. Similarly, the parable of the talents, a Sunday school "chestnut," conjures up preconditioned responses.

The plot of the parable of the talents is quite simple and very familiar to those who grew up in the pew. A wealthy master leaves money with his slaves (the Greek could also be translated as "servants") and goes away. In fact, the sums he leaves are astronomical: the first slave is left about one hundred years' salary. In spite of the tremendous burden the slaves have been given, two of them make an even greater fortune, rewarding the master's trust with enormous returns on the initial investment. Consequently, they receive great praise when their master returns. The third slave hides the master's gift and returns it

151

GOD HATES RELIGION

intact. He is scolded and rejected for laziness.

While the story is found in Luke, our memory is usually fixed on Matthew's version:

You know, it's like a man going on a trip who called his slaves and turned his valuables over to them. To the first he gave thirty thousand silver coins, to the second twelve thousand and to the third six thousand, to each in relation to his ability, and he left.

Immediately the one who had received thirty thousand silver coins went out and put the money to work; he doubled his investment.

The second also doubled his money.

But the third, who had received the smallest amount, went out, dug a hole, and hid his master's silver.

After a long absence, the slaves' master returned to settle accounts with them. The first, who had received thirty thousand silver coins came and produced an additional thirty thousand, with this report: "Master, you handed me thirty thousand silver coins; as you can see, I have made you another thirty thousand."

His master commended him: "Well done, you competent and reliable slave! You have been trustworthy in small amounts; I'll put you in charge of large amounts. Come celebrate with your master!"

The one with the twelve thousand silver coins also came and reported: "Master you handed me twelve thousand silver coins, as you can see, I have made you another twelve thousand."

His master commended him: "Well done, you competent and reliable slave! You have been trustworthy in small amounts; I'll put you in charge of large amounts. Come celebrate with your master!"

The one who had received six thousand silver coins also came and reported: "Master, I know that you drive a hard bargain, reaping where you didn't sow and gathering where you didn't scatter. Since I was afraid, I went out and buried your money in the ground. Look, here it is!"

But his master replied to him, "You incompetent and timid

SAFE CHURCH OR RISKING CHURCH?

slave! So you knew that I reap where I didn't sow and gather where I didn't scatter, did you? Then you should have taken my money to the bankers. Then when I returned I would have received my capital with interest. So take the money away from this fellow and give it to the one who has the greatest sum. In fact, to everyone who has, more will be given and then some; and from those who don't have, even what they do have will be taken away. And throw this worthless slave where it is utterly dark. Out there they'll weep and grind their teeth" (Matt. 25:14-30, SV).

From what perspective do I hear the story? If I am an over-achiever, I hear the parable as justification for my strenuous activity. The gospel seems to argue that even Jesus appreciates someone who strives for greater and greater returns on human labour. And the parable is clearly an indication that God blesses those who do, in fact, work hard. When I make my little investments double, the Creator of the universe is pleased.

When the church listens to the parable and sees itself as one of the first two servants, it congratulates itself on its growing numbers, raising taller and taller spires. That's what the reign of God is all about; making the gathering increase. And if that's what God wants, we should get out there and push to bring the lost souls into the fold. Discipleship from the point of view of the faithful servant is, therefore, the programmed increase of our investments, our missions, our congregations, and our real estate.

On the other hand, if I as an under-achiever hear the parable of the talents, my immediate reaction is anger. How unfair is this coming reign of God if those who do not produce are penalized and cast out! Surely this story is punishment to the timid and harsh medicine for the powerless. I think we could easily form a club for the unjustly treated servants of the church who have seen their best efforts scorned and misused, who, despite all their best intentions, were unable to bring any increase to the Lord's work.

There is a third perspective. Have we ever heard this story

153

GOD HATES RELIGION

from the master's point of view? Imagine, if you will, being the one who has given the money, great gifts indeed, for others to nurture. What's your point? What are you really expecting from these servants? If we think of the master in the story as a parent figure, then I believe that those of us who have been parents or functioned in a guiding role as teachers or friends could explain his expectations of those to whom he had given great gifts. He wanted his servants to take a chance with their gift. After all, gifts are to be shared, not held tight. His primary advice to the inheritors would be to give life a run for its money.

Clearly, God hates those servants who sit on their hands or who hide behind a wall of pious rationalizations feigning helplessness while evil mounts. The chief problem with an institutional religion is that it is unwilling to risk its life to correct injustice and bind up the broken-hearted. When out of self-serving fear or well-intentioned indolence the faith community remains aloof from the crises of this world that God loves, God is angered and dismayed: "You incompetent and timid slave."

It is the willingness to risk that is at the heart of the parable. The number of zeros is irrelevant in the accounting of the returned master. It doesn't matter whether we make 12,000 or 30,000 silver coins and, by extension, it would be of little consequence if we made none. The chief criteria for valuing worthiness is risk. Did you risk what you had been given in trust? That's the moral of the story.

In the final analysis, discipleship and belief in God is about taking risks for the advancement of God's reign on earth. To paraphrase Christ's words, "Woe unto us if we allow our assets, our trust funds, our real estate to grow mouldy and moth-eaten from underuse" (Matt. 6:19). Think back to the hole in the ground. How often has the church's life been dependent on risk-takers? Those Methodist ancestors saw the vision and invested their own security in making it happen.

What risk means for us at the close of twentieth century may be quite different from what it meant for those early pioneers. We may be asked to risk our reputation for the sake of the poor

154

as the social covenant on this continent is eroded and civil society disappears with it. We may be asked to risk our financial security for the homeless and our trust accounts to provide greater pastoral care to the lost. We may be called upon to risk our lifestyles for greater spiritual peace. Only as individuals and as members of a covenanted community of faith can we shape the particularities of our vision, but the universal vision never changes.

Dietrich Bonhoeffer, a martyr who resisted Nazism, maintained that true discipleship comes at great cost. So the people of the cross are called to risk. It is not an option if we want the reign of God to come.

While scepticism engendered by the many deficiencies of institutional religion may remain, I am inspired to doubt past my doubts precisely because of faithful believers who have risked all they had, who have paid the cost of discipleship in order to bring God's rule of justice and love to earth. Theirs was a wondrously spiritual and political endeavour.

Heaven help us if we fail to follow their example; heaven help us when we do.

Bibliography

Bassler, Jouette M. 1991. *God and Mammon*. Nashville: Abingdon Press.

Baum, Gregory. 1987. *Theology and Society*. New York: Paulist Press.

Brown, Raymond E. 1979. *The Birth of the Messiah*. New York: Doubleday.

———. 1994. *The Death of the Messiah*. New York: Doubleday.

Bibby, Reginald. 1987. *Fragmented Gods*. Toronto: Irwin Publishing.

———. 1993. *Unknown Gods*. Toronto: Stoddart.

———. 1994. *Unitrends*. Toronto: United Church of Canada Stewardship Services.

Bonhoeffer, Dietrich. 1959. *The Cost of Discipleship*. London: SCM Press.

Borg, Marcus. 1994. *Jesus in Contemporary Scholarship*. Valley Forge, Pennsylvania: Trinity Press International.

Charlesworth, James H. 1992. *Jesus and the Dead Sea Scrolls*. New York: Doubleday.

Committee on Church Worship and Ritual, ed. 1930. *The Hymnary of the United Church of Canada*. Toronto: The United Church Publishing House.

Coulson, Jessie. 1969. *The Little Oxford Dictionary*. Oxford: Clarenden Press.

Crossan, John Dominic. 1988. *The Dark Interval*. Santa Rosa, California: Polebridge Press.

———. 1991. *The Historical Jesus*. New York: HarperCollins.

———. 1992. *In Parables: The Challenge of the Historical Jesus*. Sonoma, California: Polebridge Press.

———. 1994. *Jesus: A Revolutionary Biography*. San Fransisco: HarperCollins.

———. 1995. *Who Killed Jesus*. San Francisco: HarperCollins.

Dickens, Charles. 1972. *A Christmas Carol*. London: Routledge & Kegan Paul.

Fiorenza, Elisabeth Schuessler. 1983. *In Memory of Her*. New York: Crossroad.

Fitzmyer, Joseph. 1979. *The Gospel According to Luke I-IX*. New York: Doubleday.

Funk, Robert, ed. 1991. *The Gospel of Mark: Red Letter Edition*. Santa Rosa, California: Polebridge Press.

Funk, Robert, and Roy Hoover. 1993. *The Five Gospels*. New York: Macmillan Publishing.

Funk, Robert. 1994. *Jesus as Precursor*. Santa Rosa, California: Polebridge Press.

Grant, George. 1959. *Philosophy in the Mass Age*. Montreal: The Copp Clark Publishing.

———. 1969. *Time as History*. Toronto: Canadian Broadcasting Corporation Learning Systems.

Hall, Douglas. 1987. *When You Pray: Thinking Your Way into God's World*. Valley Forge: Judson Press.

Heschel, A. 1962. *The Prophets*. Vol. 1. New York: Harper & Row.

Horsley, Richard. 1987. *Jesus and the Spiral of Violence*. San Francisco: Harper & Row.

———. 1989. *The Liberation of Christmas: The Infancy Narratives in Social Context*. New York: Crossroad.

Levan, Christopher. 1993. *The Dancing Steward*. Toronto: United Church Publishing House.

Mallay, Edna St. Vincent. 1956. *Collected Poems*, ed. Norma Mallay. New York: Harper & Row.

Mack, Burton L. 1988. *A Myth of Innocence: Mark and Christian Origins*. Phildelphia: Fortress Press.

McFague, Salley. 1985. *Models of God: Theology for an Ecological, Nuclear Age*. Philadelphia: Fortress Press.

Meier, John P. 1991. *A Marginal Jew*. Vol. 1. New York: Doubleday.

———. 1994. *A Marginal Jew*. Vol. 2. New York: Doubleday.

Miller, Robert, ed. 1992, 1994. *The Complete Gospels: Annotated Scholars Version*. Santa Rosa, California: Polebridge Press.

Newson, Carol, and Sharon Ringe. 1992. *The Women's Bible Commentary*. Louisville: Westminster/John Knox.

Niebuhr, Reinhold. 1952. *The Irony of American History*. New York: Charles Scribner's Sons.

Parkard, William. 1988. *Evangelism in America from Tents to T.V.* New York: Paragon House.

Schaberg, Jane. 1987. *The Illegitimacy of Jesus.* San Francisco: Harper & Row.

Schmidt, Daryl D. 1990. *The Gospel of Mark.* Santa Rosa, California: Polebridge Press.

Schumacher, E. F. 1973. *Small is Beautiful.* New York: Harper & Row.

Spong, John Shelby. 1992. *Born of a Woman.* New York: Harper San Francisco.

Tillich, Paul. 1948. *The Protestant Era.* Chicago: University of Chicago Press.

Zeitlin, Irving M. 1988. *Jesus and the Judaism of His Time.* Cambridge: Polity Press.

Also of interest from
The United Church Publishing House

The Dancing Steward: Exploring Christian Stewardship Lifestyles
Christopher Levan
How can we break free of the reigning possessive spirit of our North American culture and let go in Christian stewardship? In these financially and spiritually "tight" times, our inability to give is more than just a reflex of greed, according to noted theologian and writer Chris Levan. Questions at the end of each chapter make this a versatile and creative teaching guide for exploring the nature of Christian stewardship lifestyles.

The Future of the Church: Where Are We Headed?
Douglas John Hall
Douglas John Hall offers us a personal look at the United Church through the eyes of one who finds himself at just about the same age. Doug Hall calls this work "a biographical testimony," and uses his personal experience for the larger purpose of illustrating a more expansive analysis of our ecclesiastical sojourn.

The Man in the Scarlet Robe: Two Thousand Years of Searching for Jesus
Michael McAteer and Michael Steinhauser
Veteran journalist McAteer and New Testament scholar Steinhauser are both fascinated by one of history's most influential figures—Jesus of Nazareth— and intrigued by the current popular interest in the mystery surrounding his personality. They team up in this volume to offer us a comprehensive view of the controversies surrounding the search for the historical Jesus, a search that began almost two thousand years ago.

The Future of the Bible: Beyond Liberalism and Literalism
Gerald T. Sheppard
An entirely fresh recovery of the Bible as scripture is emerging around us. The older choice between liberalism and literalism is both misleading and obsolete. New insights will change the way the Bible speaks in matters of faith and conduct, including current controversies in the church. A timely, illuminating, challenging, stimulating book for all the people of the United Church.

ALSO OF INTEREST

Opening the Scriptures: A Journey through the Stories
and Symbols of the Bible
George Johnston
From New Testament scholar George Johnston comes an up-to-date introduction to the Bible with a clear and easy-to-follow style. Using art, literature,
politics, and personal life situations, Johnston brings the Scriptures to life in a
way that has meaning for today's reader. With illustrations, maps, charts, a
guide to signs and symbols, an annotated bibliography, and an index, this is a
unique guide for the solitary reader or discussion groups.

The Storyteller's Companion to the Bible Series
edited by Michael E. Williams
This series shows how to read and retell the stories of the Bible more effective-
ly. Each book features background information on each narrative, as well as
imaginative retellings using dramatic monologues and modern parables.
These volumes have proven to be helpful companions for ministers and
Christian educators as they prepare a text for retelling. Titles in the series—
Volume One: Genesis; Volume Two: Exodus; Volume Three: Judges-Kings;
Volume Four: Old Testament Women; Volume Five: Old Testament Wisdom;
Volume Seven: The Prophets II.

The Prophets Speak
Helen Hobbs
This is a companion to the VISION TV series, *The Prophets Speak*, which was
produced to encourage serious reflective Bible study. Each chapter offers
information, insight, and elaboration on the life and times of those whose
thinking has profoundly influenced the understanding of God in both Jewish
and Christian communities.

Faith-full Stories: The Narrative Road to Religion
John C. Hoffman
Why stories? Because everyone loves telling a story or listening to a riveting
tale. Stories are a crucial part of religious teaching, a pleasing way of convey-
ing truth from one generation to another. Which story? A religious vision
must speak to our world to offer healing. But is the story true or merely
wishful thinking? Hoffman guides us in determining a story's meaning and
testing its truth—by listening to others tell *their* stories.

Walking the Way: Christian Ethics as a Guide
Terence R. Anderson
A recognized scholar and activist in moral and ethical issues, Terence Anderson invites the reader to think about Christian ethics as a method of discerning the way to live well in a perplexing world. His focus is on "right relations"
rather than solutions, and he states that Christian ethics is not about rules and
techniques but about love and hope, about habits of the heart. This engaging
and personal volume, complete with stories and charts, is an ideal introduction to reflecting on the Christian way.

ALSO OF INTEREST

Faithstyles in Congregations: Living Together in a Christian Community
Wilena G. Brown
Faith can be a binding or dividing force, depending on the "style" in which a congregation practices it. This book provides an analysis of three faithstyles—community, searching, and partnership—found within all our congregations. Understanding the needs of each style can bring fruitful harmony and an appreciation of the gifts that each offers. A valuable aid for church leaders, outreach committee members, and all who engage in congregational life.

A Faith to Live By: A Resource for Adult Study
Frederick A. Styles
Styles investigates the challenge of faith and what it has to say about the living of our lives today. This volume explores Creeds, God, Jesus Christ, the Holy Spirit, sin and salvation, the church, the Bible, baptism, communion, life after death, and humanity. Other chapters touch on sexuality, conflict within the church, the environment, and being another's "keeper." Programme notes by Marion Pardy round out this helpful study aid.

The Double Vision: Language and Meaning in Religion
Northrop Frye
The late Northrop Frye characterized his last book as "a shorter and more accessible version of *The Great Code* and its sequel, *Words with Power*." In four very readable, engaging chapters, Frye, a minister in The United Church of Canada, condenses and clarifies the ideas and concepts introduced in those well-known earlier books and presents them in a simpler context for the general reader.

950353